Best Wishes
and
Enjoy!
Barbara Morris

CRAZY FOR CATS

Barbara Bradlyn Morris

GOLLEHON BOOKS™
GRAND RAPIDS, MICHIGAN

ISBN 0-914839-66-7
(International Standard Book Number)

GOLLEHON BOOKS are published by: Gollehon Press, Inc.,
6157 28th St. SE, Grand Rapids, MI 49546.

GOLLEHON BOOKS are available in quantity purchases; contact
Special Sales. Gollehon does not accept unsolicited manuscripts. Brief
book proposals are reviewed.

Contents

1. Max, The Mad Balcony Cat 1
2. The Kitten Who Came In A Satchel 12
3. The Battle Of The Wills 20
4. The Kitten Who Ruined Romance 28
5. How Did We Love You?
   Let Us Count The Ways 36
6. The Tiny Paw Prints On Our Hearts 43
7. It's Raining Cats! 50
8. A Case Of Mistaken Identity 58
9. The Incredible Kitty-Litter Caper 67
10. Singing The Boarding-Out Blues 77
11. The Amazing "Comeback" Cats 85
12. Masters Of The Art Of Escape 96
13. The Cuckoo Clock Caper 103
14. We Are Adopted! 115
15. An Oscar Award-Winning Performance . . 127
16. "We Are Siamese... If You Please" 136
17. It Takes Two To Travel 145
18. If This Is Hawaii, Where Are The
    Hula Dancers? 157
19. A Toast To Taiho! 167
20. We Rescue A Damsel In Distress 171
21. Showdown At The O.K. Corral! 181
22. A Shampoo And Blow-dry, Please 189
23. A Glimpse Into The Future? 199
24. Somewhere, Under The Rainbow 209
25. Cats Do The Darndest Things! 219
26. Dried Fish And Cherry Blossoms 230
27. Grow Old Along With Me,
    The Best Is Yet To Be 238

Acknowledgments

I want to give my heartfelt thanks to John Gollehon, my editor and publisher, for his enthusiasm and insight. His expertise has been invaluable, and his moral support a great gift.

And to breeder Kathy Nicholas, who so graciously allowed John to photograph her kittens for the cover. The little darlings look as if they were holding their pose for the perfect picture. Well, not exactly. As John told me later, "It's a good thing I took two rolls of film. Those little guys wouldn't sit still for one nanosecond!"

I had warned him to make sure he uses fast film!

A Primer On Siamese

Within the breed of Siamese cats, whose body colors range from shades of white, cream, ivory, and fawn, there are varieties of cats who are identified by the color of their points—that is, their faces or masks, ears, legs, feet, and tails. These points come in many colors, including red and cream, but the four so-called "classic" colors are seal, chocolate, blue, and lilac. The points of a seal-point Siamese are as dark and rich as bittersweet chocolate, in contrast to chocolate-point Siamese whose color is softer, milkier. The points of a blue-point Siamese may be light blue or a misty dark blue shade, while the points of a lilac Siamese are a frosty, pinkish-gray. All are lovely, but my husband and I gave our hearts to seal-point Siamese, who are considered to be the most extroverted and independent—as we can certainly attest to!

The origin of Siamese cats is lost in the mists of time, unknown and mysterious, which is probably as it should be since the cats themselves are cloaked in an aura of mystery—that is, when they're not being playful chatterboxes, as you'll see in this story.

Some historians think that Siamese resulted from breeding Egyptian cats with wild cats from eastern countries. But that's only an educated guess. It's not until the 14th century in Siam (now Thailand) that we find some clues—pawprints, as it were—about the Siamese cat's history. These ancient clues are poems and drawings which reveal that these beautiful cats were living in Siam at that time. However, they weren't just hanging around like ordinary cats; they were living in the lap of luxury in the palaces of kings, where they were adored and considered to be sacred. Only royal families were allowed to own them. Legends speak of the cats, adorned with jewel-encrusted collars, serving as honored guardians of the sacred temples.

Dedicated to my husband, Ward, who introduced me to the joy and beauty of cats and who shared with me the fun, the laughter, the occasional sorrow, and the constant love in our lives with our wonderful cats:

Max, Petrouchka (Pah troosh' kah), Neunsig (Noin' sig), Donner, Tristan (Tris' tan), Taiho (Ty' ho), Mikko (Mee' ko), and Maile (My' lee)

With thanks to God

One

Max, The Mad Balcony Cat

My love affair with cats began, ironically, with a cantankerous Siamese who hated me at first sight. I met him 37 years ago in Germany when my husband, Ward, came home one day with an arm-load of mean-eyed, tough-talkin' cat who took one look at me and glared a warning not to come one inch closer. I suspect that he sensed that I didn't know anything about cats—and didn't especially care for them.

We were in the bleak seaport of Bremerhaven because Ward, a Navy Lieutenant, had been ordered there a month after our marriage.

Our government housing—grim rows of concrete apartment buildings—squatted on a tract of barren land. Each of the apartments was faced with a small, iron-barred balcony, and that's where I suddenly re-called seeing this cat—on the balcony of a building across the street. I had noticed him because he seemed to be there all the time, a lonely figure, even in the dreariest weather.

"Isn't this the balcony cat?" I asked. "What's he doing here?"

"He's ours for a week!" Ward announced. "The Prestons are going to Munich so I offered to cat-sit," he explained. "I thought it would be a good way to introduce you to Siamese cats. They're really different. Great personalities. Talkative. Kind of dog-like. You'll love this cat. You'll see."

Good grief, was my husband a cat person? Did he intend to get a Siamese of our own? I did not recall this being in our marriage vows.

Ward put the cat down and patted his rear end. The animal smiled up with a look of adoration worthy of the shepherds and wise men. Then, as if to say, *I haven't forgotten you, lady*, he flashed me a sullen glance.

"Take him back, please," I begged. "I don't care about cats."

"Too late. The Prestons left this morning." Ward's grin was sly. *Too sly*, I thought.

By now, the cat was sensuously winding and re-winding his body around Ward's legs while tossing challenging looks at me. I have since learned that with those caressing motions he was marking Ward with his scent. At that moment my husband became that cat's property! Clearly sensing my defeat, with another loving glance at Ward, the big cat swaggered to the sofa, sprawled languorously, yawned, and went to sleep.

Ward beamed.

I scowled. "Well, since we're stuck with him, I better get to know him," I said. "I assume that he has a name."

Ward's smile faded. He shook his head. "Would you believe they 'haven't gotten around' to naming him? Incredible, isn't it?" His voice hardened. "I don't know why they even bother owning a cat."

Just then something happened in my heart—a tiny tug of a heartstring, a stirring of pity for a creature whose owners had put him out on the balcony alone all day and hadn't cared enough to give him a name.

"Well," I said, the growl in my voice weakening. "We can't have him hanging around here for a week without a name. Any ideas?"

Ward gave me a broad smile and a quick hug. "What do you think about 'Max'?"

"Hmmmm." I thought about it. "Max" had a big, tough sound to it. "Fine," I agreed. "He sort of looks like a Max."

Ward bent to stroke the newly christened cat. "Max, old boy," he murmured, "we're going to have a great week."

Max stirred and, I swear, he grinned and winked conspiratorially at Ward. Then he stretched grandly and settled by easy stages into a more comfortable position. Even I had to admit that he was astonishingly graceful and beautiful. He was large—at least 13 or 14 pounds—and had typical, handsome, seal-point Siamese features; his legs, tail, face, and ears were as rich and brown as fudge. His body was sleek and tubular, and his tapering, wedge-shaped face was set with vivid blue, almond eyes that gleamed with intelligence.

We decided that Max should make the first overtures to me, so, that evening, I stood aside as Ward fed him. Until then, my vision of a cat at dinner was of a quick, pink tongue lapping up a saucer of cream. Max quickly shattered that image as he chomped and slurped through a huge bowl of tuna-flavored nuggets with noisy gusto, followed by a leisurely bath. I'd never seen a cat bathe and was amazed by his thoroughness.

After smacking his lips, Max licked his right paw until it was good-and-wet. Then, with the paw curled with baroque grace, he rubbed it in languid but firm circles over the right side of his head from behind his ears down to his cheeks and chin. He repeated this pattern with his left paw on the left side. Throughout the washing, his eyes were closed in a combination of concentration and utter bliss.

Then, with stretches, bends, and archings as supple as a ballet dancer's, he licked long and industriously down his front legs, his shoulders, flanks, genitals, hind legs and, with long, sinuous movements of his head and neck, he licked his tail from base to tip. He completed his bath with vigorous nibblings between his outstretched claws.

I was spellbound by Max's impressive display of impeccable grooming—and amused by his casual attitude when he occasionally glanced our way with a look that seemed to say, *But, of course, I know I'm the very picture of exquisite feline grace.*

For the rest of the evening Max ignored me. On his way to the litter-box he made a wide detour around my chair. Mostly he lay on the sofa, next to Ward, blinking his eyelids slowly in contentment and allowing his tummy to be stroked and his ears scratched. From time to time he'd sigh, wriggle with happiness, and murmur words of love to Ward.

"See what I mean about his needing TLC?" Ward asked. "I don't think he's had this much attention in his whole life."

Max did seem starved for love. I smiled at his pleasure, and to my surprise I realized that I was almost glad that Ward had brought him in from the cold, if only for a week, and I chuckled at the effect he had on Ward, who was as happy as only a cat person can be when offered a special feline friendship.

At bedtime, Max strolled to the bedroom, curled up in the bend of Ward's legs, and fell asleep, with a limp paw flung casually over one eye and his chin propped on Ward's calf. I felt another tug of a heartstring, for, despite his bulk and tough demeanor, there was something appealing, almost angelic, about Max in repose. Instinctively, I reached out to stroke him—and was stopped cold by a keen eye that flew open and shot me a killer glance.

I flushed—embarrassed to be so openly rejected. By a cat!

"Give him time," Ward said. "He's been here just a few hours."

"Hmmph!" I snorted. "He *adores* you already. Do you know how humiliating it is to be snubbed by a mangy cat?"

"He is *not* mangy," Ward stoutly defended Max. "He just needs a good brushing." As if he understood, Max lazily lifted his head and, once again, gazed adoringly at his hero.

In the morning, to speed the process of Max's falling in love with me, I fed him his breakfast. "Here you are, Max. It looks delicious," I chirped. I'm convinced that the cat harrumphed with disgust at my forced gaiety before burying his head in the bowl .

I was uneasy, even a bit fearful, when Ward went off to work, leaving Max and me to forge a relationship. "Be good to Barbara," Ward ordered as he patted Max good-bye. "I want her to become a cat person."

"Cat person! Ha!" I said. But Ward was gone.

Max and I turned to one another, and I swear that his eyes were glowing with ill will. I wouldn't have been surprised if he'd snarled *It's no good screaming, lady. No one can hear you.*

"Well, Max, come on," I said feebly attempting cheeriness. "You can help me make the bed."

I was encouraged when Max trotted after me. Feeling foolish but following Ward's advice, I talked constantly to reassure the cat of my friendship. "Good old Max. Did you enjoy your breakfast? Would you like a catnip mouse? Ward's going to buy one." As I plumped the pillows, "good old Max" watched me intently but remained as still as the cat guardians of ancient royal tombs.

And then it happened. When I picked up the corners of the sheet and billowed it to air it out, Max turned into a growling, flying projectile. In one, swift leap he launched himself into the sheet and, with a nasty hiss, swiped his claws down my forearm.

"My gosh, Max!" I cried. I dropped the sheet and snatched up a tissue to staunch the springing rivulets of blood. I was shaken and chilled all over, never having been attacked by an animal before. All I could think was to get Max out of the room. I reached for the blanket, hoping to sweep him off the bed with it, but, once again, the moment that I moved, he lashed out. I jumped away just in time. Trembling and dabbing at my scratches, I stared, dumbfounded, at Max who crouched in the middle of the bed, unblinking and immobile—and terrifying to me.

As the tense minutes went by and Max made no further move, I began to calm down. I tried to analyze what had happened. "What's wrong, Max?" I whispered. "Did you think I was destroying your spot on the bed? Are you that insecure? If you are, I feel sorry for you. I really do." Max glowered. His eyes were wide, the dilated pupils as black as beads of ebony. The relentless swish of his tail was fearsome. Edging backward, I slipped out of the room. For the rest of the morning, each time I peeked in to check on him, Max remained crouched on the bed, as if guarding it.

When Ward returned for lunch, bearing the gift of a catnip mouse, Max was transformed. With graceful, welcoming bounds, he leaped to greet his lord and master, and, with raucous meows, reported on the distressing events of the morning. He dramatized his tale with fearful, flickering glances at me.

As Ward scratched behind Max's ears, he pondered the reason for his attack. Ward's theory was more logical than mine: Sometime in the past, someone had hit Max, and my suddenly upraised arms had rekindled that memory. "I think he was scared and defended himself," Ward said.

"That makes more sense, and it makes you wonder what kind of life this poor cat has had," I said.

Ward smiled. "You've known him for 24 hours and already you're calling him 'this poor cat'—the very cat who attacked you. And you don't think you have the makings of a cat person?"

"Hmmph. Just because I feel sorry for a poor, mistreated creature doesn't make me a cat person," I retorted.

"We'll see," Ward murmured. "We'll see."

As we sat on the sofa after dinner, Ward put Max on his lap and, with great care, brushed and polished his matted and shedding coat. Max adored it. He sighed and stretched out so long and luxuriously that his muscles actually vibrated. *More*, he murmured. *More*.

"Listen, he's purring," Ward whispered.

With a wary eye on those lethal paws, I leaned over to listen. Max peered at me through slitted eyes, but, miracle of miracles, he lay quietly and continued purring.

"Oh my!" I exclaimed with a rush of delight. "Would you believe it—I've never been close enough to a cat to hear it purr? It's fantastic!"

Ward just smiled with a hint of smugness.

For the rest of the week I left the bed unmade except for one morning when I changed the sheets. I closed the door while I did it, but, incredibly, I felt that by shutting Max out I was being rude to him. Rude to a *cat!* When I sheepishly confessed this to Ward, again he grinned that smug, I-told-you-so grin.

Little by little, Max and I developed a truce. I chatted to him constantly and plied him with gourmet treats (he quickly acquired a fancy for Jarlsberg cheese). In return, Max softened his sharp glances and stopped making detours around me, though he still did not let me pet him. On the third day, he ambled into the kitchen and politely watched me make meatballs. To my surprise, I discovered that his quiet company was most pleasant. A cat in the kitchen seemed to make it cozier.

As for Ward and Max, they were besotted with one another. The cat groveled, mewed, and purred for Ward, his hero, who had brought him in from the balcony to romp and play, to share his bed, and supply him with catnip mice.

On Max's last night, Ward was pensive as he lightly stroked the cat's upturned tummy. Max was taking one of his many catnaps on his back. His curled paws framed his head like the tiny fists of a sleeping baby. It was a pose of such innocence that I felt a surge of protectiveness toward him, and I realized how restful a room can be when it is graced by a sleeping cat.

Ward broke the silence with a whisper heavy with regret. "It'll be hard to give him back."

"Hmmmm." Despite my budding feelings of tenderness toward Max, I was still a bit non-committal.

"Come on, rub his tummy," Ward coaxed.

"Are you kidding? He'll never let me."

"Try."

Tentatively I extended my fingertips—and flashed a smile of surprise at the discovery of the plump warmth and downiness of Max's tummy.

Maybe Max sensed the solemnness of his last night; maybe he felt that he owed me a bit of gratitude. Whatever it was, instead of attacking, he opened his eyes, turned lazily, rested his chin on my lap—and began to purr. When, gingerly, I scratched behind his ears, he pushed up the volume.

That did it. All week—barring that one, frightening episode, for which I thought that I understood the reason—Max's presence had been slowly winning me over. The apartment seemed more homelike with a cat lolling about. Now, in these few minutes of tenderness with a handsome Siamese who graciously deigned to let me pet him—and tuck him into my heart—I finally felt some faint stirrings of a cat person.

The next day the house seemed unbearably empty. When we looked over at the balcony across the way, our hearts broke. For there was Max, sitting on a folding chair, staring out at the bleak street. He sat, tall and erect, head high, as if warning the world not to pity his isolation. He played the role of proud individualist to perfection, and we applauded him for it. But in our hearts we knew that, if given half a chance,

Max would collapse like a rag doll for a few moments of love and tenderness.

Max eventually moved on with the Prestons and was lost to us. However, for 37 years we have remembered him fondly, for it was, thanks to him, that I discovered the joy of owning a cat—or, more to the point, being owned by one. Shortly after Max went home, we decided to get a kitten, for I found myself longing to lavish love on a kitten, to give it the TLC that Max had craved—and was denied.

"It must be a Siamese," Ward insisted. "Didn't Max prove that Siamese are the most wonderful cats on earth?"

"Yeah, right," I grinned back.

And so it began—The Great Siamese Kitten Search.

Two

The Kitten Who
Popped From A Satchel

If there were any Siamese kittens in Bremerhaven, we certainly couldn't find them. The city's one pet shop sold only birds and fish. The Germans were renowned animal lovers—so where were all the dogs and cats?

"For dogs and cats you must go to *Frau* Schmidt," one of the German ladies in my Intercultural Women's Club told me. "From a breeder she will order for you a nice kitten."

So, on a late summer afternoon I found myself searching for *Frau* Schmidt's shop on a narrow, cobblestone street of bleak tenement houses and small stores. I finally spied it, tucked between a tiny sausage maker's shop and a tinier bakery. *Frau* Schmidt's was the tiniest—and most run-down—shop of all. It had no sign; I identified it by a battered animal crate and a heap of canned dog food in the dingy window.

Warily, I entered. It was a gloomy, narrow room that reeked of stale urine. It was furnished with a dusty wooden counter on which lay a jumble of leashes, dog collars, and rusted tins of flea powder. Crates and boxes were stacked haphazardly in the semi-darkness at the far end. When I shut the door, a jangling bell set off a cacophony of growls and yips in the crates, and an indistinct figure—*Frau* Schmidt—emerged from the murky shadows.

I gasped. I couldn't help it. The woman was an ancient crone from a Dickens' novel, short and frumpish, swathed in a shabby black cape and crowned with a sprawling top-knot of faded hair. In broken, accented English she asked, "You look for dog? *Ya?*"

"*Nein… nein..* A kitten," I stammered. "A Siamese kitten."

By combining my meager German and creative body language with her fractured English, we communicated fairly well. I learned that Siamese kittens were scarce. It might take several weeks to locate one. "Go," she ordered. "I call when ready. Okay?"

I felt frustrated. I had expected to have a kitten that day, but realizing that this disheveled woman was my only link to a Siamese cat breeder, I nodded "okay" and left.

Outside, I glanced back through the grimy window. *Frau* Schmidt was hunched over a dog-eared ledger.

The search for our Siamese kitten had begun.

Three weeks dragged by before *Frau* Schmidt called. She had a "little Siamese girl kitten—*sehr schön.*" Very pretty. She would deliver it that night.

During the three-week wait, we had studied the one cat book available in the base library. Unfortunately, it was long on cat pictures but short on cat care. My parents, in Massachusetts, volunteered to find something more practical.

We were as excited as parents with a new baby. Everything was ready: A bright-yellow food and water dish was tucked into a corner of the kitchen, a blanket-lined box made a snug bed, and the kitty-litter was as smooth and inviting as a Japanese sand garden.

Ward shot me an I-told-you-so smile as I kept vigil for *Frau* Schmidt at the window, for, as he had predicted, it had taken just one week for Max, quirky though he was, to captivate me. Moreover, the sight of him romping and snuggling with Ward had impressed me with the pleasures of owning a loving pet. Now I was eager to cuddle our own little kitten.

Though I had described *Frau* Schmidt to Ward, still, he was stunned when she arrived—a "squat munchkin" (his description) in voluminous black cape, scuffed boots, and a shapeless black fedora jammed on her bramblebush hair. She clutched an old-fashioned, black satchel patched with duct tape.

"*Guten abend,*" she rasped as she scuttled into the room and hoisted herself onto the sofa. I cringed when she plopped the grimy satchel on our pale green cushions. Was the kitten in that horrible bag?

"The kitten? You have the kitten?" My voice was impatient.

"*Ya, ya!*" she croaked. For "*Ein hundert*—one hundred—marks."

Ward and I exchanged uneasy glances. One hundred marks. That was twenty-five American dollars—ten dollars more than we had allocated for a kitten from Ward's slim, junior-officer paycheck.

Frau Schmidt noticed our hesitation. Quickly—and very shrewdly—with a flourish she snapped open the satchel.

For a moment I thought it was empty. But then, with the unique, eardrum-splitting screech of a Siamese cat, the world's most adorable kitten popped up. Her pink, rosebud mouth was open so wide that it hid most of her face. How full of sound and fury she was at being hauled around in a bag! As we watched, this blazing-mad little creature, still grumbling about her cavalier treatment, scrambled out of the satchel and slid clumsily down its slope. Her landing was wobbly-kneed, but she seemed pleased with it because she stopped bawling and looked around with a satisfied air.

Oblivious to *Frau* Schmidt's hand extended for her hundred marks, Ward and I marveled at the kitten's beauty. Her blue eyes were incredibly wide. In time they would deepen to azure and become more almond-shaped. Whereas Max's coat had been a blend of deep cream and chocolate brown, the kitten's fur was pale ivory with a dusting of light mocha on her ears, paws, and tail. Her tiny body with its gawky legs held a hint of the slim, long-limbed and elegant cat that she would become.

Once again, Ward and I exchanged glances, but these were glances of silent agreement. We had fallen in love at first sight. Of course we'd pay the hundred marks. What was mere money compared to this delightful, sassy kitten?

We thrust the marks at *Frau* Schmidt and escorted her to the door with an impatient *Auf wiedersehen*.

"A strange woman," I commented as we watched her short, stout figure clump off down the street. Although she had brought us a splendid kitten, I was glad that our dealings with her were over. I shuddered at the memory of her dark, cluttered shop and her grimy, cat-carrying satchel. I quickly put the woman out of my mind as we turned back to the kitten.

"She's so tiny!" I exclaimed and dropped to my knees to reach for her. But Ward stopped me. "First, extend your hand very slowly so she doesn't feel threatened," he advised.

I will never forget that first contact. For long moments the kitten studied my hand. Then, gingerly, she stretched her neck, millimeter by millimeter—and sniffed my fingertips with a feather-light touch of her nose! It was a moment so gentle that I melted.

Just as gingerly I moved my hand upward toward her head. Momentarily she froze. Then, as I scratched ever-so-lightly behind her ears, she tipped her head toward me as if to say, *Oh, my! I love that. More, please.*

Her immediate trust seemed miraculous. "Oh, Ward!" I sighed.

When Ward reached out to pet her, instead of merely lowering her head, the kitten plopped on her side—a clear invitation for a tummy rub. Shades of Max! (I've since learned that all dogs and cats have instant rapport with Ward: They joyfully fling themselves at him.)

But enough ear scratching for now, the kitten decided. It was time to explore this new world. On long, gangly legs she trotted to the edge of the sofa—and nearly plunged over the side. Instinctively we reached to catch her, but, she caught herself and doggedly hung on. Lowering her tiny rear end to act as an anchor, she inched her front paws over the edge of the cushion. Clearly she was dying to jump, but, bold though she was, the height was daunting. Ears twitching, she clung, undecided and tottering at the edge.

Ward laughed. "Here, little one, you could use some help." Gently he lowered her to the carpet.

The gesture surprised her. She looked shocked to suddenly find herself on a wide-open expanse with two large humans looming above her. Gone was her bravura as she scooted for refuge under the sofa—and huddled there despite our pleading, cooing, cajoling, and offering tempting bits of cat food.

"We're frightening her," Ward finally said. "She'll come out in her own sweet time."

He was right, but it was three hours before her pink nose finally made its appearance, and she slunk out, belly low, ever so slowly. Once out, however, her curiosity took over. She began to explore, warily at first, crouched low, ears pricked, and the tip of her nose twitching, but soon with increasing confidence. There were, after all, so many nooks and crannies to be investigated, so many strange objects to be sniffed, batted, chewed, or conquered with sudden, leaping attacks.

The tassels on the drapery cords had to be buffeted; the throw rug had to be flipped over and crawled under; the shoes in Ward's closet had to be stalked, swooped upon, and sniffed down into the toe; their laces needed to be chewed, batted, and tangled. The kitty-litter had to be dug into and used (thank goodness she knew what it was for!) before being flamboyantly flung about. Ward and I had to be periodically checked to make sure we were still there in case she needed a quick chin scratch. Lastly, a ball of crumpled wax paper had to be beaten into submission with ferocious attacks that were a combination of stiff-legged hops, stealthy belly-to-the-floor ambushes, and a relentless battering of paws until both the paper ball and the kitten lay limp on the carpet. Within moments, in an abandoned sprawl, our little warrior was sound asleep.

I clasped my hands. "She's wonderful!" I cried. "What do you think we should name her?"

Once again Ward was ready. "How about 'Petrouchka'?"

"Petrouchka." Thoughtfully I repeated it. Petrouchka was a lively puppet in one of our favorite ballets. The kitten's stiff-legged prancing had mimicked the puppet's bewitching, dance-like movements. "Petrouchka," I said again. "Perfect."

Petrouchka didn't flutter an eyelid when we tucked her into her bed and kissed her lightly on the forehead.

Suddenly, the reality of what we had done hit me. We owned a cat! Impulsively I wrapped Ward in a bear hug. "Guess what?" I asked with a laugh. "I think I'm a genuine cat person!"

Ward's wry smile answered for him—"I knew it all along."

I looked down at the slumbering kitten. Like all sleeping babies, she looked angelic. I knew, however, that, like all babies, she'd need lots of care. "I hope my parents send the cat book soon," I whispered. "I suspect we have a lot to learn."

Portentous words. It didn't take too many days of life with Petrouchka to realize just how much we did have to learn.

Three

The Battle Of
The Wills

Petrouchka should have come with training wheels. Almost everything we know about cat care we learned through trial and error with that spunky little kitten.

I had dreamed that life with Petrouchka would be enchanted, that we'd cavort and cuddle. Instead, it was more like a nightmare, mainly because, although Ward and I overflowed with love, we had no experience in caring for a cat. Poor Petrouchka. She paid for our mistakes with tummy aches, nausea, and bouts of diarrhea—hardly conducive to cavorting and cuddling.

Part of the problem was that we expressed our love by lavishing her with treats. When she tapped our ankles with her paw, her charm was irresistible. How could we say "no" when her limpid blue eyes pleaded for another tidbit—tidbits that were too fatty for her digestive system. When she scorned her kitten chow and demanded liver—*medium rare, please*—we catered to her as if we were in service to a princess. Thinking back, I'm astonished by our spinelessness. She, a mere furry handful, was dictating the menu!

Dr. Armmand, the Army veterinarian, scolded me roundly. "You can't keep feeding her liver. It's much too rich. Her diet needs variety and balance."

"It's all she'll eat," I argued. "I gave her a little as a treat, and now she's hooked."

"Then unhook her."

"How?" My voice rose in frustration. "I've tried everything. She absolutely refuses cat food. If I don't give her liver, she'll starve."

"She won't. Believe me, she won't," he assured me. "Hold out for two or three days. She'll come around. She's got to learn who's boss!"

Two or three days without food! How could we do that to her? On the other hand, it broke our hearts to see Petrouchka's tiny body exhausted by diarrhea. When I damp-wiped her tiny rump, it pained me to see how sore and reddened it was.

So began the battle of wills. Three times a day I spooned fresh cat food into Petrouchka's bowl. "Din-din, Petrouchka!" I called out gaily and made yummy licking sounds to tempt her. Three times a day she sniffed, turned up her nose, and stalked off. Once she even made scooping motions over the food with her paw exactly the way that she scooped kitty-litter to cover her mess in the litter-box. The message was clear: *That's what I think of your cat food!*

In the middle of day two, Petrouchka changed tactics. Instead of stalking off, she sat and stared at me from the exact center of the room as if she knew that she looked particularly small and isolated there. For one so young and inexperienced, she had a high sense of drama. Her pathetic look spoke volumes. *I'm a poor, starving kitten. Liver, please*, it pleaded. *Medium rare.*

"I can't, Petrouchka, I can't! It's for your own good." I turned away in tears.

It was a hellish time. Ward and I felt like brutes. Imagining Petrouchka's hunger pains, we suffered with her. We couldn't concentrate. Couldn't read. Couldn't play Scrabble. We slept fitfully. Every time Petrouchka went toward the kitchen, we tip-toed after her. But she only sipped water.

Then, on the morning of the third day, when, bleary-eyed, I stumbled out of bed to check the food dish, I found it empty! Licked clean! Nearby, Petrouchka was washing her face with an unflappable air.

I fell to my knees beside her. "Trushkie, you ate!" I cried. "Ward! Come quick! Look! Trushkie ate!" (From that moment on, the spontaneous and endearing nickname of "Trushkie" stuck.)

I might as well have been far off in the Gobi desert for all the heed that Trushkie paid me as she licked her curled paw, then smoothed it over her face to wipe away stray crumbs. Her calmness admonished me. *No need to get so excited. Okay, I lost the battle. I admit it, but look how graciously I'm accepting it.* Taken in by her nonchalance, and, being a novice cat owner, I didn't realize that her half-closed eyes harbored a look that warned of battles yet to come—battles she intended to win.

Gradually, as we learned more about cat care, Trushkie regained her health. On a diet of cat food mixed with powdered vitamins and sprinkled with shredded wheat for added fiber, she became a tiny tornado swirling through the apartment as if fireworks were exploding inside her, and, of course, she expected me to join her lively games.

Forget the housework, she'd chirp and invite me to a game of hide-and-seek by crouching at the doorway with only her nose peeking out. Tensely she'd wait— how agitatedly her ears would twitch!—until I passed. Then, bushy tailed, she became The Pouncer! Oh, she was ferocious, pummeling my calves with her paws before suddenly dancing clownishly away, on stiffened legs, in a sidewise, crab-like motion.

I never got to be The Pouncer, for the moment that our roles were reversed and Trushkie was the one to be pounced upon, her imagination took flight. She seemed terrified of being The Pouncee. All her bombast would collapse. Crying pitifully, she would skulk to my hiding place, flop sideways in an "I give up" position, and declare the game *called for a tummy rub*.

We thought it was miraculous that Trushkie had such a strong body and delightful personality because everything in her background should have worked against her. According to our well-thumbed cat book, in order to develop emotional stability, kittens should remain with their mothers for eight or nine weeks. We got Trushkie when she was only seven weeks old. Furthermore, we learned that kittens should be handled gently by many people in order to socialize them. Considering that Trushkie had been carted around in a dilapidated satchel, we doubted that she'd been gently handled and encouraged to be sociable. One factor was in her favor: The many noises she'd been exposed to— at the breeders, on the train to Bremerhaven, and amid the yapping dogs in *Frau* Schmidt's shop—had taught her that strange noises are not necessarily threatening. As a result, Trushkie took in stride our jangling door bell, our "fire station" alarm clock, and the floor poundings of "Old Rattles," our ancient washing machine. She even slept through the eardrum-shattering, atonal squalling of German police sirens.

While our friends with new babies buried their noses in Dr. Spock, we diligently plowed through the cat-care book that my parents had sent. I don't remember its name. We just called it "The Book," and we quoted it like holy writ. It alerted us to ear mites, taught us to clip claws, terrified us with descriptions of feline enteritis (a disease as tragic as the plague, as we would one day discover) and amazed us with the fact that Siamese cats don't like milk. Trushkie wouldn't touch a drop, and, until we read The Book, we were convinced that, lacking in calcium, she would become bowlegged or hunchbacked from rickets or osteoporosis.

Thanks also to The Book, we learned why Trushkie had ignored our welcome gift of a catnip mouse. After a few sniffs and idle bats with her paw, to our chagrin, she had turned back to her favorite toy—a fascinating ball of crumpled wax paper.

"Well! So much for our gift!" Ward exclaimed. "Ungrateful kitten," he teased her. "Whoever heard of a cat that ignores catnip?"

Shortly after that I found the answer in The Book: "Kittens under eight weeks usually are not turned on by catnip." So, Trushkie wasn't an ingrate after all. She was just too young. "In another week she'll probably go bananas over it," I remarked. Little did I realize how prophetic my words were—nor how much we'd soon want to pitch that little mouse out of the window.

As if she, too, had been studying The Book, two days after Trushkie turned nine weeks old, she dragged the mouse from under the sofa—and, she did go bananas. As though possessed, she tossed and batted it, rolled sillily back and forth on it, stalked, pounced, and captured it. She took it in her teeth and, growling, tried to shake it to death. She lay on her back, balancing and tossing it in her paws like a circus bear with a beach ball, then wrestled with it as mightily as if it were a multi-armed sea monster. Finally, she stood on her hind legs and swatted it with the skill and fervor of a volleyball champ. The mouse flew high, landed on Ward's chair, and slipped down behind the cushion.

Trushkie spun around, her eyes darting. Where was it? She feinted right, then left, then plopped down on her rump and emitted a small bewildered mew.

"The poor little thing is puzzled. Give it to her," I urged Ward.

"Ugh. It's all chewed and wet." Ward grimaced. "Here, Trushkie! You're welcome to it!" He tossed it across the room.

I had heard of greased lightning, but that was the first time I saw it. Trushkie was up and flying across the room before Ward finished his sentence, hurtling with such speed that she zoomed past the mouse, sailed off the carpet, skidded across the floor, and caromed off the wall before crashing to a halt.

"Ouch!" I cried, but, rising in a flash, Trushkie hardly noticed. When, at last, she cornered the mouse, she danced over it like a victorious prize-fighter. Then swaggering triumphantly back to Ward with it, she deposited it at his feet with a satisfied look that asked, *Don't you just love gifts of mice?*

"She retrieved it!" I exclaimed. "The Book says that some cats can be trained to retrieve if you give them a reward."

Ward was intrigued. "Let's try! Trushkie seems like a good candidate." He tossed the mouse again.

Once again Trushkie flashed across the room, did her victory dance, and flounced back with her gift for Ward. She did it again. And again—each time offering it to Ward as proudly as a knight laying war trophies before his king.

"She doesn't need a reward," Ward marveled. "She's a natural-born retriever."

"She's also exhausted," I noted. "Give her a rest."

That evening we celebrated Trushkie's talent with a bottle of *Liebfraumilch*. "To Trushkie the Retriever!" we cheered. Trushkie missed the celebration—she was curled in her box, sleeping off her exhausting day. I stroked her cheek and whispered a goodnight on my way to bed. "See you in the morning, sleepyhead."

But we didn't have to wait until morning. Five minutes later, with the mouse clamped in her jaws, Trushkie leaped onto the bed, trotted to Ward's chest, and dropped the mouse on it with an engaging grin that challenged him to a return match.

Chuckling, Ward told her, "Just once, then we've got to sleep."

But Trushkie didn't give a fig for our sleep. She had discovered her purpose in life and nothing was going to stop her. When Ward hid the mouse under his pillow and pointedly turned away from her, she burrowed feverishly for it, dragged it out—and dropped it on my chest.

I laughed. "Okay, but just for a few minutes."

Ten minutes later, as Trushkie retrieved the mouse for at least the fifteenth time, I called a halt by putting it out of her reach atop the high bureau.

I fell asleep to the background sounds of Trushkie's frustrated cries as, over and over, she tried to jump to the top of the bureau—but fell back with soft thuds to the carpet, time after time.

Sighing, I buried my head under the pillow and made a mental note to check The Book. Hopefully, it included a chapter on "How To Stop A Kitten From Retrieving."

Four

The Kitten Who Ruined Romance

We had come to Germany eager to visit the charming villages, magnificent museums, and medieval castles that beckoned us. Now that we had Trushkie, we planned to take her with us, but first we had to accustom her to car travel—a challenging task, for her trips back and forth to the vet had always been in a cage—and always with her screaming at top volume. We wanted her to enjoy life on the open road without a cage—and serene instead of screaming.

We began with four-or five-minute excursions and gradually made increasingly longer trips. I held Trushkie—or tried to—while Ward drove. The first rides were adventures in terror as Trushkie screeched, clawed, and stiffened her body with incredible strength. It was a battle royal in which I could barely keep a grip on her. On our fifth trip, suddenly she stopped squirming. She looked squarely at the two of us as the light dawned on her that we could be trusted, that we wanted her to have fun. *We always brought her home in time for a good dinner, didn't we? So, why not relax and enjoy the passing scene?*

Once Trushkie made that decision, she did an about-face with the precision of a Marine drill instructor. She became a traveling cat without equal. She discovered that there were great views to be had from Ward's shoulder. She'd perch there for hours as he drove, taking in the beauty of northern Germany's lush apple orchards and sheep pastures. We celebrated her transformation into a Dedicated Car Cat when, on a trip to Hanover, she leisurely lunched and used the kitty-litter while hurtling down the autobahn at 80 miles an hour!

The next question was: Could we train Trushkie to a leash so she could explore on foot with us? "Of course," said The Book. "With time and patience, many cats can be trained to a leash." Time. Patience. Ha! Those two words should have been in bold print and underlined.

To accustom Trushkie to having something around her neck, during one of her happy, tummy-rubbing trances, we slipped a narrow, bright-red collar over her head.

What's this? She opened her eyes, narrowed them with a quizzical look, and shivered her shoulders before deciding that whatever this new thing was, it was okay. It was lightweight, and, equally important, it didn't interfere with scratching behind the ears and under the chin. After a quick exploratory sniff at the collar, she let her eyelids droop and sank back into sweet oblivion.

We let out our breath.

During the following days we attached progressively longer and heavier lengths of string to the collar. Trushkie not only tolerated them, she played with them, chasing the ends round and round. In our innocence, we high-fived one another. This leash training was a snap!

Oh, yeah, muttered Trushkie the next day when, instead of string, we attached a leash to the collar. It dangled temptingly, but this time Trushkie didn't play games. Instinct told her that something was up. This was "the real thing." She balked. She hunched. She refused to move.

"This behavior is normal," said The Book. "Attach the leash to the collar several times a day for 15 minutes each time until the cat accepts it."

Even after all these years, the memory of those fifteen-minute sessions is etched permanently on my brain. Pointedly ignoring the leash and hunkered down so low to the carpet that she seemed to melt into it, Trushkie glared at us, her eyes dark with reproach: *I thought you were my friends. I trusted you. I became a car cat for you. Why do you torment me this way?* If she had intended to bury me in guilt and break my heart, she succeeded. "She's going to hate us forever," I wailed. "Let's give up."

But Ward was made of sterner stuff. "We have to show her who's boss," he declared, echoing the vet and The Book. "Let's try tempting her with treats." But even when we held out her favorite tidbits, Trushkie refused to approach us to get them.

On the fourth day, sensing that she was in a losing battle with Ward, by degrees, Trushkie moved two feet toward the cheese that Ward held in his hand. But oh, how dramatically she moved! Knees bent low, head straining forward, eyes slitted, stomach skimming the carpet, she glided in slow motion as if she were hauling a back-breaking weight. I felt like applauding; this was melodramatic acting on a grand scale.

For two more days, Trushkie crept and slunk, bearing her dreadful burden—until quite suddenly, without warning, she tired of the whole affair. *How tedious*, she seemed to sigh. *Enough's enough. You win, Ward*, she added in a gracious manner and rose in majesty to promenade around the house trailing her leash as nonchalantly as an actress swathed in a feather boa.

In her own kooky fashion, not only did Trushkie accept the leash, but she became a *vain* leash cat! Perhaps she glimpsed herself in the mirror one morning, for one day she suddenly seemed to realize that her red collar and leash were *très chic*. She took to prancing, head high, with a jaunty air that delighted the animal-loving Germans who fawned over her when we walked in the park. With Trushkie's approval, Ward lengthened the leash with a sixteen-foot-long cord. This allowed Trushkie to trot far ahead of us, legs pistoning in high, light steps, nose in the air, eyes flashing and glancing around for admiring Germans. Clearly, she knew that when she pranced down the street like a fancy drum majorette she looked absolutely smashing. Did a more charmingly vain kitten ever trod this earth?

By the time of our first wedding anniversary, Trushkie was a charming, outgoing five-month-old kitten who was fast developing the tapering lines of a typical Siamese. And, like all good Siamese, oh, could she talk! Depending on her mood, she prattled, chirruped, babbled, chortled, mumbled, howled, squawked, bellowed, wailed, scolded, or screeched. Whatever her chatter, it was definitely not to be ignored. Being Siamese-cat fanatics, Ward and I were proud of her wide range of conversational tones and loved to show her off. So, we were eager to take her along on our anniversary celebration in *Schloss* Arensburg, an ancient ruined castle that had been converted into a romantic, hilltop inn. "Will Trushkie be welcome?" we asked when we called to make reservations. "But of course," came the reply. "We're Germans, aren't we? We love cats!"

On our arrival, the entire staff of the inn, including cook and dishwasher, crowded into the lobby to welcome Trushkie. Shamelessly she batted her eyelashes at the cook, frisked with the tips of the manager's shoelaces, presented her tummy for tickling by the housekeeper and chirruped sweet compliments to all. Well, besides being vain, she was flirtatious! The staff was charmed. We began to suspect that Trushkie's mother had been an irresistible coquette.

Our room, in the castle's stone tower at the top of a spiral staircase, was breathtakingly lovely. Surely it had been decorated by Germany's answer to Laura

Ashley. We were engulfed in blooms. Masses of flowers burst forth from vases; patterns of roses and ca-
mellias overflowed the walls, cushions, and bedspread,
their colors glowing richly in the soft pink light of silk-
shaded lamps. There was a three-foot-thick eiderdown
quilt on the end of the bed patterned in a tapestry of
violets and rosebuds. We sighed. We adored every blos-
soming inch of it. It was a room for romance, a room
in which to play Chopin Nocturnes, to read love sonnets, and to sip champagne from a lover's slipper—the
perfect room to celebrate a first anniversary.

Trushkie agreed. She seemed as smitten as we were
and gave us a look of rapture when we put her kitty-
litter box under the sink and tucked a spray of baby's
breath in it.

Then Trushkie found one more thing to adore—
the feather quilt. She took one look—and leaped. And
disappeared, sunk deep in the downy quilt.

A moment later her happy face popped into view.
Just as she had thought—the quilt was a cloud-soft
trampoline! With a joyous squeal she leaped again. And
again. From puff to puff, she appeared and disappeared
in the eiderdown. Soon, with insistent cries she begged
us to join the fun.

And so we invented the game of "Toss Trushkie."
It was quite simple: We took turns, gently tossing
Trushkie through the air into the puffy quilt where
she'd sink out of sight, then scramble triumphantly to
the crest of the billows and mew mightily for more.

But soon the castle's dinner chimes called softly.
We scooped cat food into Trushkie's dish, dressed in

our best cocktail clothes, and, in a cloud of perfume and after-shave, descended the spiral staircase as elegantly as Scarlett and Rhett.

Obviously the staff had spread the word of the young American couple—and their delightful kitten—on their first anniversary, for we basked in the smiles of the other guests in the intimate, candlelit dining room.

We began with paté and champagne, sipped from crystal flutes. A fairy tale anniversary in a fairy-tale castle.

Then, in the middle of the Salade Composé, featuring warm Brie and toasted almonds, it happened: The Cry.

The blood-chilling howls of wolves in the deep Arctic night are mere canary trills compared with the high wail that suddenly spiraled down the staircase that magic night. It split the air. It rose and fell in eerie, spine-tingling waves.

It was useless to look startled and pretend that it was a castle ghost. Siamese cries are as distinctive as fingerprints. This was Trushkie—and everyone knew it. Smiles faded. The maitre d'hotel frowned.

"I'll go," I whispered and dashed up the spiral stairs at Olympic speed.

Trushkie was like a tiny, wild thing, standing defiantly on the bed, her mouth wide open and screaming. The instant I burst into the room, she stopped in mid-howl and plunged toward me, an excited gleam in her eye. Her body language clearly demanded: *Let's play "Toss Trushkie."*

So I tossed. And tossed some more.

Trushkie bounded and rebounded, insanely, maniacally happy—until I stopped and headed cautiously for the door. And again she screamed. And screamed.

I went back to Tossing Trushkie.

We ate our meal in shifts. When Ward finished his lonely Salade Composé, he filled in for me in the Trushkie Toss. When I finished my lonely filet mignon, I took his place. Where did a five-month-old kitten get all that energy? It was like a baton relay race, with Trushkie as the baton.

Gone was our moonlight walk on the terrace. Gone the after-dinner drinks by the fire. Gone was romance. We were exhausted and irritable.

When, about nine o'clock, Trushkie finally tired of the game, she dropped lightly to the floor and, in ladylike fashion, ate her dinner—uninterrupted, of course. When she finished and had bathed to her satisfaction, she thanked us for the marvelous evening by blissfully pummeling our ankles with her head.

We smiled wearily and sank to the floor to cuddle her. "What can you do with a cat like this?" I asked Ward with a helpless shrug.

"Not much," he admitted, "except to laugh, love her—and keep on tossing."

Five

How Did We Love You? Let Us Count The Ways

On the Friday after our unique anniversary celebration, I tucked Trushkie into her carrying case and drove her, flaming mad, to the Army vet, to be spayed.

"It's okay, it's okay. It's only for one night," I said. But Trushkie knew that the carrying case meant going to the vet's, and she wanted out.

I took deep, calming breaths. Although The Book assured us that spaying was routine, I dreaded the thought of Trushkie being anesthetized, then awakening in pain in strange surroundings. Ward hid his worry by talking glibly about it. However, I noticed that before leaving for work, instead of his usual farewell pat on Trushkie's rump, he picked her up to rub noses and whisper good-bye.

When we entered the medicinal-smelling clinic, Trushkie notched up her decibels, braced herself on stiffened legs, and thrust her shoulders repeatedly against the bars. Her dilated pupils looked black and fathomless. If the vet's assistant had not appeared at that moment, I would have turned and run. As she reached for the case, I was suddenly hit hard by the realization that I couldn't stay to stroke and comfort Trushkie while the vet treated her. Reluctantly, I handed over the case.

"Don't worry," the young woman said gently. "It's routine. We'll call you as soon as the operation is over."

When Trushkie realized that she'd been taken from me, her cries dwindled to whimpers, and she seemed to collapse. My last sight of her was of a huddled figure whose eyes, behind the bars, implored me to rescue her.

I drove home slowly, haunted by that pleading look.

Ward called twice. "No word yet," I barked at him. I was edgy, and I jumped at each telephone ring. Finally, in mid-afternoon the vet called.

"How is she?" I cried. "When can she come home?"

The long silence before he cleared his throat to speak sent a chill up my arms.

"Mrs. Morris," he began, then paused for what seemed ages. "I'm sorry… I have sad news… Trushkie had a reaction to the anesthetic… she didn't make it. Her heart… it gave out during the operation."

My body sank in on itself. I had the sensation of crumpling in every part—my gut, my cheeks, even my eye sockets.

"No-o-o!" My grief escaped in a forlorn wail. "No, no, not Trushkie," I moaned.

"This happens. It's extremely rare... but it can happen. For some reason her little body couldn't take the strain. I am so very, very sorry."

I barely heard him. My head pounded with the shock of death. Never to see that sweet kitten again! The thought was totally, absolutely unbearable.

Somehow, in a daze but guided by the doctor, I accepted his offer to cremate Trushkie. I agreed it was best not to see her but to remember her sparkling with life.

When I hung up, I raised my head and howled. Tears, welling like freshets, soaked my cheeks, neck, and shoulders. Finally, drained and hoarse, I collapsed on the sofa. I took a deep shuddering breath; I had to call Ward.

When, in a broken voice, I whispered the news, he was so silent I thought we'd been disconnected. Then, tersely, he murmured "I'll be right home."

When, ten minutes later, he hurried through the door, we held one another for a long time, crying, confused, disbelieving.

At dinner, as we picked at an omelet, we kept expecting to see Trushkie, delicately raised on her haunches, pawing softly at our arms, begging, with irresistible charm, for a bit of Swiss cheese. The sight of her water dish and food bowl choked me with tears, and I wept when I stroked the hollow that her body had made in "her cushion" on the sofa. But saddest was bedtime, when we realized that we'd never again feel her light leap to our chests, never see the gleam in her eyes and the eager tensing of her muscles as she played "toss and retrieve" with her beloved catnip mouse.

"I can't stand it! I know that we can't replace Trushkie, but we need to get another kitten as soon as possible," I sobbed.

Ward nodded. "First thing in the morning we'll go to see *Frau* Schmidt."

I groaned. "Do we have to? I hate that grungy shop—and it takes her so long to find a kitten." Then, without thinking clearly, I burst out, "Let's go to Hamburg! It's big. There's got to be a real pet store there!"

The idea was insane, and ordinarily Ward would have told me so, but in his grief, he, too, ignored reality. Spurred by this faint, desperate hope, both of us had sudden visions of a dear kitten awaiting us in Hamburg, a large city fewer than two hours by car from Bremerhaven.

Knowing that railroad stations are the hub of most German cities, we decided to begin our search the next morning at the Hamburg station. There might even be a pet shop right there!

"We can look in the Yellow Pages!" I said, wracking my brain for every possibility.

Our plan, which was completely unrealistic and impractical, denied several facts: We did not know Hamburg; all we had was a small, sketchy map; I spoke only halting "tourist German," and even if Yellow Pages existed, we wouldn't be able to read them. However, in our sorrow and the need to take immediate action, we closed our minds to anything that might stand in our way.

The next day, as we neared the city, our search at first seemed charmed. A man who was walking a dog told us, in halting English, about a large, well-known pet shop—Fockleman's at the railroad station. We set off with high hopes but discovered that Hamburg was undergoing extensive urban renewal projects. The streets were a maze of barricades, ditches, and detours. By the time we found a place to park, it was noon. Our nerves were fraying.

"Fockleman, Fockleman," we repeated, circling the station, scanning the shops.

Nothing. We circled again. Still nothing.

Next we tried the nearby streets. In vain. In desperation I began to stop people right and left. "Fockleman?" I pleaded, proffering my map.

No one spoke English, but everyone nodded vigorously at the mention of Fockleman. "*Ya, ya, Fockleman,*" they echoed eagerly, and marked their version of the route on our map.

Each time, our hopes were renewed, but each time, we came to dug-up streets and incomprehensible (to us) detour signs.

Then, suddenly, there it was! Fockleman! We rushed in—then stopped short and groaned. The "large, well-known" shop was only slightly larger than our apartment! It was alive with hundreds of twittering birds, and brilliantly colored fish in gurgling aquariums.

But nary a cat. Nor a dog. Not even a hamster.

That was the first of many frustrations and disappointments as we spent the afternoon criss-crossing the city in search of other pet shops. We got lost, back-tracked, made illegal U-turns, and blindly followed detours around Hamburg's many waterways. Helped by a young woman with borderline English, we found two more pet shops, but, again, there were only birds and fish. We even found the local animal shelter, the *Tier Heim*. Our hearts melted as we gazed into stacks of cages of homeless adult cats who rubbed back and forth against the bars and meowed for our attention. It was heartbreaking. I ached for them and wished I could scoop them all up and take them home. Ward saw the temptation in my eyes and tugged at my sleeve. "We can't care for every cat in the world, Barbara," he whispered. "Come on, let's find just one Siamese kitten."

The teen-age volunteer at the *Tier Heim* offered one last hope. In stilted but correct English he said that a cultural exchange organization called America House might know about cat breeders. At least they could make phone inquiries for us. "However, America House is on the opposite side of Hamburg," he added apologetically. We groaned but headed back into the maze of streets.

We found America House in the middle of a major construction area. The closest parking was three blocks away. To get to the building, we balanced on narrow boards spanning the torn-up sidewalks—and found a sign on the door that delivered the bad news in both German and English: "Closed for two weeks, due to construction."

I sagged against Ward and fought tears. "I can't believe it! We've tried so hard," I cried. Ward hugged me close as we tramped dejectedly back to the car.

As if nature itself were mocking our frantic, helter-skelter search, halfway there the air suddenly darkened with monstrous black clouds that released a hard, chilling rain that flattened our clothes to our bodies and churned the earth into shoe-sucking mud.

The storm was as brief as it was violent. Three minutes later, the sky was a clean azure, streaked with the gold of the late-afternoon sun. Still shivering and wet, we viewed the rain as a wake-up to reality; we'd been crazy to think that we could find a kitten by trudging through the streets of Hamburg.

We drove out of town, past vineyards and orchards, on a charming, cobblestone, country road, beneath the arches of beech trees and white birch. Trushkie would have loved the view. I glanced at Ward's shoulder and felt a pang. It looked barren without her perched there.

The soft blanket that we had intended for the new kitten lay on my lap, a reminder of our failure and our loneliness. I glanced at Ward. He drove steadily, silently, his cheek moist, his mouth tightly pursed, as if to hold in his sorrow.

"I guess it's back to *Frau* Schmidt," I sighed.

Ward nodded, and his voice cracked. "First thing, Monday morning," he agreed.

Six

Tiny Paw Prints
On Our Hearts

When, with the help of my German dictionary, I tearfully told *Frau* Schmidt of Trushkie's death, I was touched when her rheumy eyes softened, and her knotted hand patted my arm with surprising gentleness. At my plea for another kitten, *"Sehr schnell, bitte*... very quickly, please," she nodded so vigorously that her frazzled topknot slid from its precarious moorings.

"Ya, Ya... bald, bald... soon, soon," she promised.

Eight days later she and her satchel were at our door. From the first moment I sensed that something was amiss. Instead of bustling in, she held back, wizened and withdrawn in the folds of her ancient black cape.

"Come in, come in!" we urged.

She did, but paused before unlatching the bag. "Kitten *ist etwas klein*... a little small," she muttered. "Maybe a little sick... a cold... sneezing."

All cats sneeze from time to time, so why this subtle warning in her tone? Ward and I exchanged puzzled frowns.

"*Ya, ya, Frau Schmidt,*" I urged her. "But please, let's see the kitten."

As she popped the latch, we leaned over, eager to glimpse the kitten who was probably just as infuriated by captivity as Trushkie had been. But when the bag yawned open, there was no sound, no movement.

Alarmed (had the kitten suffocated?), we peered into the dimness, and, with sinking hearts, made out a small, pale, huddled shape.

Instinctively I reached out, but *Frau* Schmidt nudged me aside to plunge her arm into the bag and retrieve a tiny, trembling kitten—so small that it fit perfectly in her cupped hand.

"*Klein,*" she said unnecessarily. "But nice. *Sehr schön.*" She set the tiny creature on the carpet. "Special price. Ninety marks—*Neunzig marks.* Twenty-two American dollars," she announced with a sly glance to judge our reaction.

The "special price" kitten remained hunched and motionless.

"My God, what's wrong?" I cried as Ward and I dropped down beside her.

"*Frau* Schmidt, this isn't just a cold," Ward said sternly.

"*Ya.* A cold. Be okay soon," the old woman insisted.

My heart went out to this dear little creature who could not have been more than six weeks old. Her dull, spiky fur was the milky-white shade of a baby Siamese with hints of color, like pale bruises, on her ear tips and tail. She was drawn into a ball, her head drooping, her paws tucked tightly, and her thin tail curled close. She stared unseeing through cloudy, half-lidded eyes.

"Maybe it's the flu," I suggested. Her bony fore-head looked as fragile as porcelain. I touched it with my finger tip, but even so light a caress sent her into shivering spasms.

I bit my lips to hold in a sob. This was so different from what we'd visualized. Still grieving deeply for Trushkie, we'd dreamed of an enchanting kitten to fill our empty hearts. Instead, this helpless creature was so tiny and pathetic that my heart ached even more. I longed to cuddle and soothe her as if that would mi-raculously restore her health.

Ward guessed my thoughts. "We can't take her, Barbara." He was gentle but firm. "Be realistic. This is a really sick kitten."

"But it could be flu!" I insisted. "And the vet can help that, can't he?"

We were speaking too quickly for *Frau* Schmidt to understand everything, but she caught the word "vet."

"*Ya!* Vet!" she cried. "You take to vet. No pay to-day. Pay later."

"That seems fair," I said.

Ward sighed, his emotions as ragged as mine.

"If we don't take her to the vet, she'll go back into the satchel and to that smelly shop," I persisted.

"Oh, God!" Ward's shoulders sagged. "All right," he finally agreed. "Take her to the vet in the morn-ing."

When *Frau* Schmidt had scurried out looking relieved, as gently as possible I nestled the kitten in a shoe box lined with soft flannel. Once again she shivered painfully at my touch, and, with great effort, she inched backward to tuck herself, as small as possible, into a corner of the box. She turned her head aside at my offer of water and bits of cat food.

For hours we sat quietly by her, our hearts aching, watching for her slightest movement. At midnight, Ward reluctantly went to bed. He had an early morning meeting. His sympathetic touch on my shoulder as he whispered "good night" cracked the dam of my welled-up tears.

Exhausted, I lay on the carpet, my face just inches from the kitten. Without thinking, I began to murmur over and over, "Dear, sweet, little *Neunzig*, please open your eyes… sip some water… respond in some way, please, little *Neunzig*."

Which is how *Neunzig* got her name—as simple as that. It was the German word for "ninety," the number of marks that *Frau* Schmidt had asked for her. It came, unbidden, in my jumbled thoughts and prayers.

Dozing fitfully, I stayed there until dawn. When, once or twice, *Neunzig* stirred, I held my breath with hope, but it was only the slight shifting of her paws.

In the middle of the night I did something which, even after all these years, makes me feel ashamed. In the desperate hope that *Neunzig* might move if she weren't confined in the box, I lifted her onto the carpet. I think I was expecting—hoping—that she'd miraculously stretch out a bit and show some sign of strength. But all I did was cause her pain, and, once again send her into spasms. Under my fingertips the tremblings of her thin, pale skin felt like the flutterings of butterfly wings.

Neunzig did move, but not as I had hoped. Instead, inch by painful inch, she dragged herself back to the box and struggled to climb back to her corner nook. It may have been the only soft, secure place she'd ever known.

Blinded by tears and utterly ashamed of my thoughtlessness, I eased her back into place, then collapsed, emotionally exhausted, next to her. I didn't stir until Ward came to check on both of us at sunrise.

It was particularly painful to carry *Neunzig's* box to the veterinary clinic that morning for I had had my last glimpse of Trushkie there ten days earlier. Now, after examining *Neunzig*, the vet cursed and drummed the air with his fist.

"Sorry for the outburst," he said a moment later, "but, seeing a kitten like this infuriates me. She should have been isolated—and probably should have been euthanized."

At my baffled look, he gave me the terrible news. *Neunzig* had either feline enteritis or feline peritonitis. Both were extremely infectious and deadly diseases. Without testing and bloodwork, he couldn't tell exactly which disease it was, but both were invariably fatal, especially to very young kittens. "This little thing will probably not last the day," he said sadly.

"Oh, no!" I moaned and sank into a chair.

"I see red when breeders and dealers sell these pitiful animals to unsuspecting buyers," the vet said. He
stroked *Neunzig's* head with a fingertip. She was too
sick to even shiver. "Take her back," he advised me.
His voice was low and sympathetic. "Since she doesn't
belong to us we don't have the right to put her down.
All we can do is hope that she won't suffer much longer.

"Oh, one more thing," he called as I headed for
the door. "Just in case it is peritonitis, disinfect your
apartment thoroughly and—I hate having to tell you
this—don't bring in another cat for six months. A good
six months. I can't stress that enough." He patted my
shoulder. "You've had a rough time lately," he said. "I'm
truly sorry."

I nodded my thanks, my throat too choked to speak.

I drove very slowly to *Frau* Schmidt's. I didn't want
to jostle *Neunzig*. Also, I was putting off the moment
when I would have to leave her in that horrid shop.
My vision was blurred by tears, and in my anger and
helplessness, like the vet, I wanted to lash out with my
fists.

Frau Schmidt had the grace to look sheepish when
she saw the huddled kitten. She even seemed truly
moved when I told her that *Neunzig* only had hours to
live. I made her promise not to put her in a cage or
satchel. It seemed the least I could do to ease *Neunzig's*
misery.

She nodded, then hesitantly asked if we wanted
another kitten. I shook my head and, as best I could in
faltering German, I told her about the six-month waiting period. My heart was like a stone in my chest as I

bent over *Neunzig* to whisper a trembling good-bye in her tiny, shell-pink ear.

At that moment, my sadness overpowered the anger that raged in me when I thought of the breeder who had taken *Neunzig* from her mother, to be sold at only six weeks of age even though she was obviously suffering. I was also angry and disillusioned with *Frau* Schmidt for her willingness to sell *Neunzig* if we'd been foolish enough (as I had almost been) to take her in the hope of curing her.

Trushkie's death and *Neunzig's* illness were my first experiences with the pain and death of lovely, living creatures. If any good came from their deaths, it's that they made me more aware, more compassionate toward sick, helpless animals who must trust humans to care for them and do what's best.

As for tiny *Neunzig*, we've taken some comfort in knowing that we pillowed her pain-racked body as snugly as possible on soft white flannel to provide her with a small haven. We prayed that she sensed the love with which we surrounded her for the short time she was with us.

That evening as we mourned both Trushkie and *Neunzig*, we suddenly realized that once again, like Max, we had given two needy creatures a name—names that defined them and gave them personality. Largely because of *Neunzig's* name, which, to us, sums up her sad story, that dear little kitten lives on very clearly, very dearly, in our memory.

Seven

It's Raining Cats!

"Except for his small wound—and that should heal quickly—this is one fine kitten!" Dr. Armmand made the joyful announcement after examining the pet that Ward and I had waited six long months for.

"Thank God!" My pent-up breath escaped in a huge sigh. We had agreed to buy the kitten from *Frau* Schmidt on the condition that we get the vet's approval. Now the doctor and I grinned at this perky little charmer who, purring as smoothly as a Mercedes, gazed at us with such sweet friendliness you'd think he had just been given a taste treat instead of a vaccination for feline distemper.

"I think you've got a winner, Barbara," Dr. Armmand continued. "His fur is glossy and silken, his ears are clean. Looks like he's had good care. And though it's too early to be 100-percent sure, he seems amazingly well-adjusted."

I nodded and smiled, but a small worry lurked in the back of my mind. It was that wound, that small patch of black skin, on the kitten's shoulder. When I'd asked *Frau* Schmidt about it, she shrugged it off, explaining that when the kitten's two littermates were sold, mama cat abruptly tired of her maternal duties and refused to let the last kitten—our kitten—nestle with her. Each time he tried, she nipped his shoulder and shoved him away. The image of that rejection was heartbreaking. Although Dr. Armmand assured me that the wound would heal and that fur would cover the scar, I wondered about a possible scar on the kitten's psyche? Bitten and pushed aside by his own mother! Wasn't this potential for a freaked-out cat? For deep emotional scars? Dr. Armmand couldn't say. "Just flood him with love," he wisely—and unnecessarily—advised.

Now, telling the kitten what a great little guy he was, the doctor scratched him behind the ears—and was rewarded with top-volume purring and a goofy, heavy-lidded look of pure pleasure.

I stowed my worry temporarily and laughed. If only Ward could see that silly look, he might have second thoughts about the appropriateness of the booming, macho name he'd given the kitten—Donner, god of Thunder. Ward, an ardent opera buff, had persuaded me to name the kitten after a mythological character in Wagner's opera, *Das Rheingold. Pretty heavy stuff to unload on such a small creature*, I thought, and at this moment I seemed to be right. Our little god of Thunder, purring up a storm, looked as cuddly and lovable as a Disney drawing.

I left the clinic with Dr. Armmand's warning not to be alarmed if Donner were sluggish and refused to eat that evening. It was because of the shot; he'd soon be fine.

I placed the carrying case on the passenger seat with its window facing me so I could coo and comfort Donner if he panicked during the ride home. Panic? Apparently the word wasn't in his vocabulary. Instead, his alert, friendly gaze seemed to politely command, *Home, James.*

As I drove, exchanging pleasant looks and incessant chatter with Donner, I thought about what a truly amazing kitten he was. The day before, when I'd gotten him from *Frau* Schmidt, he'd been equally obliging. The elderly *frau* had not delivered Donner to us in her black satchel (which may have accounted for his look of bliss). Nor, despite his name, had he arrived in a thunderstorm. He did, however, arrive in a steady downpour, and as I look back on it now, more than 35 years later, I'm convinced that I was temporarily crazy to do what I did—to risk that dear kitten's health.

This is what happened.

It was noon, and it was pouring. After a quick lunch, Ward left to run errands before returning to the office. No sooner was he gone than *Frau* Schmidt called to say that she had a kitten. "Pick him up within half an hour," she ordered. After that she was closing shop for the day.

"A kitten! A kitten!" I cried.

But wait! Only one? On the recommendation of The Book that kittens need playmates, we had ordered two.

"In three days comes another cat," *Frau* Schmidt assured me.

I hung up and punched the air with my fist. "Yes-s-s-s! A kitten!"

But I only had half an hour! Where was Ward? He'd want to go with me. In two frantic phone calls, I had him paged at the Post Exchange and the Officer's Club.

"Sorry, he's not here."

"Not here, either."

I'd have to go alone. I raced down the stairs and crossed my fingers before turning the ignition key in the clunker of a car that we'd bought for running local errands. Just as I'd feared—a feeble grind, then nothing. The clunker hated rain, even gentle mists, and this was a slanting downpour, blowing in from the North Sea.

Downpour or not, by then I was so determined to get that kitten that my common sense dissolved like a sugar cube in coffee. Grabbing an umbrella, a towel, and the blanket-lined "kitten basket" that we'd prepared for this day, I sloshed off at a jog.

The kitten that awaited me on *Frau* Schmidt's counter top made me forget the stalled car and my soaking-wet feet, for the moment I stomped in from the rain he stopped in mid-play—he was dizzily trying to capture his tail—cocked his head, appraised me with wide, questioning eyes—and began to chatter—and chatter—and chatter. In just 15 seconds he told me his whole life's story and added that he'd love to go home with me where we could talk more at our leisure.

Well, we'd wanted a talkative Siamese, and this little guy filled the bill. Looking at him, I was certain of two more things: First, this little fur ball was the delightful epitome of a kittenish kitten; second, in no way was he the epitome of an elegant, prize-winning Siamese.

When they are adults, pedigreed seal-point Siamese—whose family ancestry is documented in impressive "papers"—have delicate, wedge-shaped heads, cream and fawn colored bodies, and ears, mask, legs, feet, and tail of dark brown. In kittenhood they have very pale fur that gradually darkens as they age. This kitten broke all the rules with his chunky round head and body as dark and plump as a bonbon, except for lighter mocha patches on his shoulders and tummy—a ludicrously rounded little tub of a tummy. He reminded me of a bear cub. The only "papers" he'd ever have would be the ones lining his litter box. No problem—we wanted personality, not papers.

I barely had time to question *Frau* Schmidt about the wound on his shoulder, when, eager to close her shop, she swept the kitten into my basket, tossed the towel over it and assured me that "in three days will come another kitten." With that, the little fellow and I were out the door!

Ward was scrambling from his car in front of our apartment at the same time that the kitten and I arrived. When he had finally gotten word that I'd tried to reach him in two places, he assumed I was sick. He had rushed home just in time to watch in jaw-dropped amazement as I sloshed toward him, hunched under a huge umbrella and huddled protectively over a towel-draped basket.

"We've got a kitten!" I shouted above the torrent.

Once he realized that I wasn't dying, Ward was beset by a whirl of conflicting emotions—curiosity, eagerness, joy, relief, and exasperation.

"You're crazy—absolutely crazy to run around in a rainstorm with a kitten in a basket!" he scolded as we ducked into the shelter of the doorway. "Both of you could get sick! Your feet are soaked. The kitten could be drenched!"

"Oh Ward," I chided. "Look!" I whipped away the towel. "Dry as a bone!"

Ward looked down, straight into those smiling, blue eyes—and fell in love. It was a love requited, for the kitten, prattling away and, excitedly wriggling up toward Ward, made it clear that, starting this very minute, he and Ward were buddies for life. Watching them bond, I offered a silent prayer that the kitten would pass the vet's exam in the morning.

Compared with elegant, strutting Trushkie whom we'd gotten when she was seven weeks old, and with sickly *Neunzig* who, at six weeks, was hardly bigger than a tennis ball, nine-week old Donner was solid and well-developed. In contrast to Trushkie's initial tentativeness, with a "can-do" spirit worthy of a Marine recruit, Donner immediately vaulted from the basket, hit the ground, running, and cavorted and bounced off the furniture like a rubber ball. Obviously it was his duty to explore every inch of the apartment at breakneck speed, including inside the wastepaper basket—a head-first dive into it and a wildly comic, scrambling escape.

Laughing and applauding, we watched the antics of this confident, sturdy-bodied kitten who, it seemed, could do anything. Well, almost anything—for, try as he might, he could not lie on his back; his round tummy rolled him right over again!

We worried a little about that tummy. During our six-month waiting period we'd almost memorized The Book and knew that a pot-belly could be a sign of worms. On the other hand, when we saw—and heard—Donner snort, gulp, and guzzle his way through a heaping dish of kitten chow, we were surprised that his belly wasn't twice its size. We added "tummy" to our list of questions for the vet.

The next morning when Dr. Armmand gave his verdict of "an excellent, well-adjusted kitten," he assured me that Donner's roly-poly tummy was a typical kitten thing, the result of a healthy appetite.

Healthy? Gluttonish was more like it. However, with the image of thin, wasted *Neunzig* still vivid in our memory, it was a pleasure to watch—and listen to—Donner gobble his dinner that first rainy evening. The next night, following his distemper shot, he pounced on his food with the same gusto. Sluggish? Another word not in Donner's vocabulary.

True to her word, at noon three days later *Frau* Schmidt called. A little girl kitten was waiting. When could we come for her?

"Now!" I shouted.

Ward grabbed the "kitten basket," and off we raced.

We rode in anxious silence through the narrow streets, for each of us was wondering what we'd find. Counting Max, in less than a year we'd had four emotional experiences with cats. Adventure number five was coming up. What would *Frau* Schmidt pull out of her satchel this time?

Eight

A Case Of
Mistaken Identity

When we entered the pet shop and saw the kitten perched on the counter, Ward and I stopped short and gasped. My heart did a loop-the-loop.

Could it be?… Trushkie?

Of course not. But the kitten who peered wonderingly at us could have been Trushkie's identical twin.

"It's uncanny," Ward whispered.

I nodded, speechless. This charming kitten had the same triangular face, the same pale coloring, and, in her gawky baby's body, we saw, as we had seen in Trushkie, a hint of the long-limbed and elegant cat she would become.

"*Sehr schön, ya?*" *Frau* Schmidt beamed, pleased with her discovery of this jewel.

"Oh, *sehr, sehr schön,*" I said, offering my fingertips for the kitten to sniff.

But always the business woman, *Frau* Schmidt in-
tervened. Unceremoniously, she scooped up the kitten
and plunked her in our basket. "You take first to vet,
then pay," she said.

Ward and I exchanged a quick, worried glance.
Before leaving the house, we had called the clinic and
were told that Dr. Armmand was out of the office until
Monday, four days away. Would *Frau* Schmidt agree
to wait that long for our decision—and her payment?

We needn't have worried. The woman was shrewd.
She knew that in four days we and the kitten would be
bonded like super glue.

We drove home with the kitten curled tensely at
the bottom of the basket. Her head was ducked, and
her tail covered her eyes. Trembling slightly, she
seemed mouse-shy, but when I lightly stroked her, I
felt her tension gradually ease. My heart lifted at this
hopeful sign of such a ready response to a loving touch.

"Even though she's not officially ours, we should
give her a name," I said and wasn't surprised that Ward
was ready with another name from a Wagnerian opera—the goddess Fricka. A goddess! I liked that.

I leaned over the basket. "Hi, Fricka!" I called
softly. When she raised her head to me, and once again
I saw the image of Trushkie, I was overwhelmed by
memories. Tears came to my eyes. I wiped them away.
It wasn't a time for tears. It was time to welcome this
new kitten. "Your name is Fricka, little one," I whispered. In answer, Fricka ducked her head back under
her tail as if to say we'd discuss names later—as soon
as this miserable car ride was over.

We had the best intentions of introducing the kittens exactly as The Book recommended—gradually, by separating them and letting them get acquainted by sniffing, "talking," and batting at one another's paws through the narrow space at the base of the door between them. So logical. So neat. However, I'm sure that the author of The Book never tried this with Siamese cats, a breed famous—no, infamous—for its unique strong personality, vibrant vocal chords, and eardrum-piercing cries. Within an hour, Donner's and Fricka's raucous screeching, howling, bellowing, squawking, and frantic scrabbling at the door had driven us half-mad. The Book be damned! The door must be opened!

"We've got to be ready to leap to the rescue if Donner protects his territory by attacking Fricka," Ward cautioned.

"*His* territory!" I exclaimed. "He's only been here three days!"

"He thinks it's his, believe me," Ward replied and reached for the knob.

As the door slowly opened and Fricka saw Donner standing four-square before her, she went into a tense, timid, half-crouch. We held our breath. Donner's ears, pricked and alert, twitched nervously, a sign that he was agitated. At the same time he was wagging his tail as excitedly as a friendly puppy. We relaxed and laughed. Donner's body language spoke volumes. Clearly our amiable, laid-back kitten was faced with a major conflict. Should he assert his "first cat" male dominance and launch an attack on this territorial intruder or should he playfully hurl himself at her and suggest a wild game of hide-and-seek?

He solved his problem by doing a little of each. First came a superb display of aggressive male behavior. It was such a classic display that we wondered if Donner had been reading The Book and taking his cues from it. With a low growl he chased Fricka around the room, snapping at her tail and swiping her bottom with a swift paw to inform her that this apartment was his territory and that this kind of bold, brave, masculine stuff is what she'd face if she stepped out of line.

It was quite an impressive act considering that Donner was such a cuddly bear-cub of a kitten. Fricka was certainly impressed—well, at least for the first hour. Then, she seemed to sense that at heart Donner was a softy who was aching to play. We watched in amazement as she showed us that, despite her youth, she was one shrewd little kitten, for she suddenly stopped running. Then, after kowtowing with just the right degree of humility to acknowledge Donner's territorial rights, with a rabbit-like hop, she jumped him.

Donner was jolted! But just for a moment. Then he grinned and the chase was on. He ran. He hid. She ran after him. She found him under the sofa. They tussled mightily. They nipped one another's tails and growled from time to time to show how terrifying they were. Then it was Fricka's turn to run, to hide, to be found, and, very briefly to display her tummy in a "poor little dominated me" pose. It was a clever ploy that safeguarded Donner's pride even as the game continued.

And how Donner reveled in his dominance! Head high, he straddled Fricka's submissive body in an I-am-lord-of-all-I-survey stance. But not for long, for, at heart, Donner was wildly, kittenishly excited about a new playmate, so, wisely, he didn't push his "top cat" attitude too far. For her part, Fricka was smart enough not to push for equality. She never forgot Donner's "top cat" status, and for as long as I knew them, Fricka always positioned herself to the left and slightly behind Donner—*very slightly behind*. It was her cagey way of walking the fine line between the status of "second cat" and her individual status as a personable and independent cat. Very subtly done—but Donner got the point. And she got respect from him.

Though I was unnerved by Fricka's strong resemblance to Trushkie, gradually I realized that the two cats were similar only in coloring and body shape. In demeanor and attitude they were worlds apart. Although Fricka was quick-witted and resourceful, she lacked an awareness of her charms, an awareness that Trushkie had had by the bushel load. Aflame with self-confidence, Trushkie had pranced and strutted, mindful of all admiring eyes. As graceful and lovely as Fricka was, to prance and to strut was not her style. I wondered, *would she have been more assertive and more aware of her fine appearance if she had been the first cat in the house, if she, instead of Donner, had had first claim to the territory?* Possibly. We'll never know. I doubted it. I did know that she would never equal Trushkie in saucy self-assurance. But then, what cat could?

At bedtime the exhausted kittens toppled together in their lined bed-box, propped like throw-pillows against one another. Until now Donner had ignored the box, preferring to snuggle with us. We were worried that we'd roll over and squash him. Now that he had a companion, we cheered to see both kittens in their own bed.

But we had cheered too soon. An hour later, we were jolted from sleep as the madcap twosome, led by Donner, leaped to our bed and frolicked in and out of the covers for 15 minutes. Then, as if an invisible hand had flicked the off switch, they collapsed and nestled under my chin, curled around one another, one light, one dark, like a Yin and Yang symbol.

As I fell asleep, my nose twitching in the kittens' warm fur, I prayed that Dr. Armmand would approve of Fricka, for she had won our hearts completely, not in four days but in less than four hours.

My prayer was answered. Fricka passed Dr. Armmand's exam *summa cum laude*—"an all-round great kitten!" At first she squirmed under the vet's exploring fingers, but, soothed by his admiring murmurs, she soon vibrated with a steady purr. Both she and Donner were proving to be most amiable creatures.

"Well," Dr. Armmand said concluding his exam, "This little guy has the makings of a classic seal-point Siamese—glossy fur, strong teeth, and good gums. And his bone structure is especially fine."

I beamed as if I were responsible for Fricka's superior qualities, but then quickly corrected the doctor. "'Fricka' is a girl's name. She's a goddess in an opera."

"Is that right?" the vet laughed. "Well, "Fricka" may be a girl's name, but this kitten is definitely a boy."

As I gawked in amazement, the vet gently tipped Fricka over and pointed to the tiny genitals nestled in the kitten's lush fur. "They're not obvious at this stage, but, believe me, Barbara, this is a little boy kitten." He chuckled at my open-mouthed shock. "Know any good opera names for gods?" he teased as he prepared to give Fricka her (his?) distemper shot.

That evening I broke the news to Ward with the same question. "Know any good opera names for gods, Ward? Because—listen to this!—Fricka is a male!"

Ward believed me only after I tipped Fricka over before his astonished eyes. Once again, Fricka, purring, took the tipping in stride.

Surprised, Ward sank into a chair. "That *Frau* Schmidt," he muttered. But a moment later he laughed wryly at the absurdity of our living with a kitten for four days and not noticing its sex. "Well, there's one practical benefit," he said. "It's easier, safer and cheaper to "fix" a male than a female." I nodded. That thought had also crossed my mind, especially after our tragic experience with Trushkie.

"So, what shall we call him?" Ward said, perking up. "How about "Wotan," the head of the gods? A sturdy masculine name."

"Hmmm." I thought about Wotan as I eyed Fricka who, gazing quizzically at us, was sitting in his subtle secondary position, a little behind and to the left of Donner. He was handsome and clever—a kitten to be reckoned with. But he was definitely not a Wotan, not a chief of the gods. All evening we tried out operatic male names.

Parsifal? Too noble.

Count Almaviva? Too much of a mouthful.

Boris? Boris Morris? No way.

Figaro? Too trite.

"Tristan?" Ward suggested wearily as the evening grew late. "A handsome hero."

"Tristan. Tristan and Donner. Donner and Tristan." I tried out the names in tandem. "I like it!" I declared. "And the names flow well together."

"Tristan it is, then!" Ward cried. He swooped up both kittens so quickly they squeaked tiny mews of astonishment. But then, snuggled with us on the sofa, they drifted into sleep with drowsy sighs as we stroked them and repeatedly whispered their names into their peach-fuzz-lined ears.

In his drowsy state, Tristan languidly nuzzled my hand. His nose, as cool as a dewdrop, was like a touch of velvet on my wrist. Donner tried to fight sleep with some lazy swipes of his paw at the ribbon-tie on my bathrobe, but sleepiness won out, and he soon lolled across my lap.

Gazing contentedly at our little family group, I gave silent thanks that we had followed The Book's advice to get two kittens. They had certainly doubled our delight, doubled our loving, and doubled our fun.

I sighed so deeply that it was almost a purr.

At that peaceful moment it didn't occur to me that double kittens can also mean Double Trouble—but I would find that out soon enough.

Nine

The Incredible
Kitty-Litter Caper

Double kittens meant double use of the litter-box. Thirty-seven years later, my nose still wrinkles at the memory of that box, for in those days, the litter wasn't much better than sand. For all I knew, it may have come from the banks of the nearby Weser River. Today's cats should drop to their knees in gratitude for their modern state-of-the-art, anti-bacterial, dust-free, time-release-odor-control, chemically treated litter granules that instantly bond with urine to form solid, odor-free clumps—veritable miracles of modern technology!

Our German litter not only did not clump, but when I poured it into the litter-box, it billowed into the air in clouds of gritty, pore-clogging dust that settled in a fine, beige film on the furniture. When the kittens' urine turned the sand to mud, the litter-box, molded of cheap, porous, lime-green plastic, sucked up the smelly moisture like a sponge and reeked of ammonia.

I hated that litter, but at least I didn't have to tip-toe barefoot in it as Donner and Tristan did. Meticulously clean by nature, they loathed it, and they quickly learned that the only time that the sand was 100-percent dry was immediately after I cleaned the box and refilled it. As soon as they heard the soft sizzle of fresh litter being poured, they scampered to the box—and there they sat in the swirling dust, two slit-eyed, sneezing sentinels, patiently waiting for the air to clear so they could step delicately into the litter and use it, at least once, in relatively dry, odor-free comfort. That sizzle was so compelling that it even aroused the kittens from sleep. Groggy and half awake, they would trudge to the box as if hypnotized.

Before long, the apartment and the kittens were so smelly that I was embarrassed to invite friends to visit. Our dream of double fun with double kittens was turning into an odorous nightmare.

Every day I scoured the litter-box until my fingertips ached. I really needed a sandblaster. I shot scented powders and sprays into the air until the room was as misty as dawn on the Maine coast, but they just masked the odors temporarily.

I probably imagined it, but it seemed that the smellier the kittens became, the snugglier they became. Every night we battled them as they tried to cuddle under our chins, and we pushed them, puzzled and mewing, to the bottom of the bed—and, preferably, to another room. This added a new worry: Were we giving them inferiority complexes?

Finally, Dr. Armmand came to our rescue. His advice: Buy a new litter-box, line it with a plastic bag, and pour in just one inch of litter instead of four or five inches, then change both the litter and the bag two or three times a day.

Embarrassed, we slapped our foreheads. Simple common sense! Why hadn't we thought of it? At last the box stayed dry, and the oft-changed litter was almost odorless. We whooped for joy. The kittens, ecstatic, practically purred as they peed.

Next, we tackled the odorous kittens with dry shampoo. "No water needed. Just rub the lotion gently into the kittens' fur to restore their fresh scent," the doctor said, sounding like a TV ad.

Dry shampoo! Incredible! It sounded too easy to be true. And, of course, it was.

The first hurdle was the smell of the shampoo. Not to put too fine a point on it, it stank worse than the urine. The cats took one whiff of the shampoo and flashed away, bounding over tables, vaulting chairs, and springing up on bureaus. They even tried scrambling up the slick side of the refrigerator. We streaked after them in hot pursuit.

When we finally trapped them in a death grip in the bathtub, we massaged the lotion into their fur—then jumped back in amazement as the stirred lotion sprang to life and mushroomed over the kittens' bodies like mounds of whipped marshmallow.

The kittens reacted with Shakespearean fury. They howled and flailed mightily. Their struggles sprayed the room with swirling ribbons of lotion. As the kittens gradually weakened, so did the foam. The mounds slowly collapsed into a milky gray, mucousy coating that slithered over the kittens' little bodies like an alien organism. Their fragile skeletons were starkly outlined under their drenched skin and slicked-down fur. The sight of those frail, shivering bodies made me cry, and my heart broke to see their bewildered, woebegone expressions. At that point, I wouldn't have blamed them if they'd run away from home and taken to a vagabond life on the open road.

To regain their trust, as we towel-dried them, we cooed and murmured words of love. But they weren't buying it. Ominously silent, they remained rigid with anger. Donner chose to stab our hearts with a sullen glare, while Tristan opted to drown us in guilt with a devastatingly wounded expression.

When we let them out of the bathroom, they streaked off, with their fur sticking out in damp disorderly spikes, like furious little porcupines .

All evening the kittens worked to rid themselves of the last traces of the shampoo. First, they licked, but when it foamed at their mouths, they bucked like broncos, hopping sideways and backwards, wildly flinging their heads to shake off the bubbly spittle. Next, trying to rub the dry residue off onto the carpet, they threw themselves down and rolled around as if demons were writhing under their skins.

I tried to help, but when I approached Donner with a clean towel, he shot me a hateful look that reminded me of Max. *Don't dare come an inch closer*, his glance warned. Tristan also backed off, but instead of hatred, he wounded me with a heart-piercing look of reproach. *Cruel woman. How could you have done this to kittens who worship you?* I had no idea that honest and simple little Tristan could lay the guilt on me so thick.

No one ate dinner that night. The cats were too busy grooming, spitting, and making nasty faces. Ward and I were too distraught. In bed, we lay awake a long time listening, dejectedly, as the kittens cursed and swore and continued their licking. Our diligent reading of The Book had taught us the importance of grooming. Besides waterproofing a cat's fur, continual licking maintains the fur as an insulator. Licking also helps to relieve tensions when a cat is agitated. And right now Donner and Tristan were two of the most agitated kittens in northern Germany.

"Do you think we've destroyed our closeness with them?" I asked.

"I doubt it," Ward answered. "It may take a few days, but I'm pretty sure they'll come around."

I hoped that he was right, but it was hard to imagine those two kittens ever trusting us again. As I tossed and turned, I pondered the responsibilities of owning a pet. Captivated by Donner's and Tristan's charms and still pretty new at this pet business, I hadn't been prepared for the nitty-gritty, unglamorous aspects of caring for small, helpless creatures. And I certainly had not been prepared for the occasional heartaches. Tears welled up as I remembered perky little Trushkie and fragile, fatally ill *Neunzig*. That night, my dreams were whirlwinds of furious, foam-covered kittens.

But miracles do happen! In the morning I awakened with my nose buried in the clean fur of Donner's tummy. Ward was half-smothered under Tristan's tummy. I got all teary-eyed again, this time for joy, for, without a trace of resentment, when the kittens had finished grooming, they had claimed their rightful places, snuggled under our chins, sound asleep. I uttered a soft, smiling sigh at the sight of the rosy tips of their tongues flopping out of their mouths—a sign that they were relaxed and content. It made them look totally goofy. But who cared? How many humans would be so quick to forgive and forget?

"Worms!" I shrieked.

It was a week after the dry shampoo. Cleaning the litter, I discovered that the kittens had a touch of diarrhea, which was bad enough, but my stomach flip-flopped at the tiny, pale squirming "things" in the litter-box. Worms! Disgusting, yucky worms!

I went berserk. I called Ward at work. "Worms!" I screeched.

"Calm down," he ordered sternly. "Get some deworming pills from the vet. It's not the end of the world."

"Oh, no?" I snapped. "Well, I'm the one cleaning this disgusting mess. I'm practically vomiting, and when I think of those slimy things inside the kittens, I could die," I wailed.

"Don't die. Call Dr. Armmand," Ward said. He was so calm I could have killed him.

On the phone Dr. Armmand was equally calm. "It's not unusual," he assured me. "I'll give you some deworming pills. Bring the kittens to the clinic."

I began to feel sheepish about my hysteria.

The deworming pills were bright-blue capsules. Dr. Armmand demonstrated how to pop them into the kittens' mouths, firmly but gently holding the jaws open with one hand, and, with the other, popping in the capsule, then stroking the kitten's throat to slide the pill down. It was so quick and smooth that the kittens had only one moment of wide-eyed surprise before they went back to batting at the doctor's dangling stethoscope.

I was impressed—and relieved. What a marvelous way to give a pill to a cat! The doctor sent me home with two more capsules, to be "administered" the next day.

Fortunately I "administered" the capsules in the bathroom, with the door closed. Otherwise, the whole apartment would have been spattered like a Jackson Pollock canvas, for, the instant that I touched Donner's jaw, he caught on. Something nasty was up. His eyes glinted with suspicion—and the battle was on. The tighter I grabbed him, the more he jerked away. Growling, he struggled to scootch his rigid body off my lap. Tristan, scared and bewildered, huddled in a corner, muttering low, distraught meows.

I began to sweat. I wanted to give up, but with visions of worms slithering through the kittens' insides,

I set my jaw. This pill was going to be "administered"—
or else. With my elbows as a vise around Donner's
squirming body, I pried his jaw open half an inch,
jammed the capsule past his teeth, and quickly clamped
his mouth shut. He stopped squirming instantly but
glowered as if I'd slipped him cyanide.

"Quit glaring. It's for your own good," I muttered
and stroked his throat to slide the capsule down. With
a chest-heaving sigh of relief, I let Donner jump down.
He inched backward, his fur in ruffled disarray, his fe-
verish eyes locked on mine. Then his lips thinned in a
gloating smile, and I could almost hear a fiendish *Heh*,
Heh, *Heh*, as, casually, he spit out the capsule.

"No!" I shouted and lurched for him. The struggle
continued. The capsule's gelatin coating, slippery with
saliva, softened and thinned as I repeatedly tried to
force it through Donner's clamped teeth. Finally the
inevitable happened—the capsule split. Half the liquid oozed into Donner's mouth, the rest seeped onto
his chin and chest. It was *déja vù*—the shampoo scene
all over again! Only, this time, the flying fluid was blue.
It splotched the white bathroom tiles and spread, like
veins in blue cheese, over the porcelain sink. My sweat-
soaked T-shirt, splattered with blue spittle, looked like
a Rorschach test.

After an identical struggle with Tristan, I edged out
of the bathroom and closed the door on the two furious, foaming, blue-tinged kittens. My only hope was
that, as they licked themselves, they'd swallow enough
medicine to be effective.

When Ward came home, not knowing what to expect, together we eased open the bathroom door.

Out they slunk, Donner first, followed by his shadow, Tristan. We knelt and cooed, but as far as they were concerned, we were wallpaper. Ignoring us, they turned their heads, kept their distance, and flounced past us, their tails swishing as one in angry rhythm. I've seen dancing chorus girls with less precision.

"Now we've really done it," I groaned. "They hate us—me, especially."

At the sight of the blue-spattered bathroom and the clump of soggy, blue-stained towels, Ward could imagine our skirmish. This time, even he wondered if I was right.

At dinner that night, in a desperate attempt to win back the kittens' love, I muttered, "Just once, the heck with nutrition," and blatantly bribed the kittens with their favorite snacks—cheese puffs and orange sherbet.

"You're shameless," Ward said, "Trying to win them over with treats."

"Hey, whatever works."

Something did work. Whether it was the cheese puffs or the kittens' undying affection for us, I'll never know. I know only that half-an-hour later, with a ho-hum air as if the day had been a total bore, Donner leaped lightly to the sofa, gazed at us with eyes flooded with love, and settled down, his chocolate-colored rump on Ward's lap, his solid little head on mine. Tristan quickly followed, burrowing his light-colored body in and around Donner's dark, limp form until they

looked like a giant scoop of fudge-ripple ice cream—
ice cream that purred and stretched with ecstasy when
we stroked it.

My shoulders sagged in relief. Once again, the kittens had proved to be amazingly well-adjusted. I wondered if Donner's kittenhood experience of being
spurned and snapped at by his mother was the reason
that he craved so much attention. Because of lack of
love from his mother, had he learned to appreciate every scrap of loving that came his way even if it meant
enduring bitter medicine? And did Tristan follow
Donner's lead because, as "second cat," it was the thing
to do?

Ward laughed and said that I'd been reading too
much Freud. However, he agreed that except for the
kittens' anger and hysteria over the indignities of the
shampoo and deworming—not totally unwarranted—
they were pretty even-tempered and could probably
handle whatever crisis life tossed at them.

Little did we know that, before the month was out,
the kittens would again prove that, indeed, they were
two very laid-back cats--*as long as they had their way*!

We would also discover, to our dismay, that, like
brazen hussies, they could play fast and loose with their
affections.

Ten

Singing The Boarding-Out Blues

It was late Sunday afternoon. We had just returned from a long, fun-filled weekend in Copenhagen. While Ward made a brief stop at his office, I hurried to the Army vet clinic where we had boarded the kittens. I could hardly wait to see them. This was our first time away from them, and I ached to hug them. I had missed them as much as if we had been away for three years instead of just three days.

A young soldier, an aide at the clinic, let me in the building, which, lighted only by some security lamps, was silent and deserted. However, as he escorted me to the pet-boarding area, the quiet night was suddenly riven by haunting cries that echoed through the dim hallways. I'd never heard a sound like it, even on our wedding anniversary when Trushkie's cries had reverberated through the castle. Those had been plaintive pleas for a playmate. These cries were forlorn, and they swelled with an air of desolation. Donner and Tristan? Could it be? I picked up the pace and shot an anxious glance at the soldier—but he avoided my eyes.

When we reached the large, walk-in cage, I winced, for, huddled together at the back of the cage, the kittens were howling fearfully, their heads thrown back like baby wolves.

I was stunned. I knew that Siamese cats, being gregarious, may "pine" (according to The Book) if left alone, but I had no idea that pining included such raucous, chilling cries.

I dropped to my knees, thrust my fingers through the bars of the cage and called. "Donner! Tristan! I'm here! I'm here!"

At my cry, the howls faded and the kittens blinked, momentarily confused, in my direction.

"It's me, little guys, it's me," I called softly. "I'm back."

In a flash, both pair of eyes widened with joy as they scampered to greet me. Bleating as plaintively as lost lambs—*How could you have been so cruel to leave us for so long?*—they stretched out their paws through the wire bars. Our reunion was as dramatic as the return of the doughboys to their sweethearts in World War I movies.

"Oh, my dear babies, I missed you so much," I whispered and sighed with pleasure to feel the light pats of their paws on my cheeks.

But then, startled, I drew away. Donner's right paw was crusted with dried blood, and a soiled bandage lay on the floor of the cage! At my sharp, quizzical glance, the soldier spoke hesitantly.

"Those kittens went near crazy here, ma'am. Howled mostly the whole time. And clawed at the bars. The brown one ripped his paw. The doc wasn't here so I bandaged it, but he kept chewin' it off. Chewed the blanket, too, so I took it away." We had left a blanket for the kittens' comfort and security. It was a standard Army blanket, part of the furnishings of our quarters. Now, the soldier held up the blanket. I was dumbfounded. Like khaki-colored Swiss cheese, the blanket was dotted with ragged holes of varying sizes, some as big as salad plates.

"The kittens did that?" I asked incredulously.

"Yes, ma'am. And they swallowed some of the wool. But it don't seem to have hurt 'em."

I prayed that he was right. Except for Donner's paw, they looked all right. When we opened the cage, with raspy squeaks the kittens hurtled toward me to butt their heads and twine their arched backs against my ankles.

"They're sure cute," the soldier said. "They stopped howlin' and rubbed my ankles just like that every time I went in the cage to feed 'em."

"They did?" A blade twisted in my heart. Donner and Tristan poured out their affection to every Tom, Dick, and Army corporal who fed them? After all the love we lavished on them? I felt betrayed. "Traitors," I whispered with a teasing smile. Instantly they flopped on their backs and gazed up, wide-eyed. Their looks of innocence clearly asked, *Traitors? Us? We who adore you?*

Traitors or not, who could resist them? I swooped them into my arms and carried them home to a meal of treats—not only cheese puffs and orange sherbet, but spoonfuls of rich German liverwurst over which they smacked their lips, then licked and bathed meticulously for the rest of the evening.

When, sulking, I told Ward about the kittens' loving response to the soldier, he was annoyingly logical. "Look on the bright side," he said. "We should be glad they're so adaptable."

"Adaptable?" I said. "They howled, they ate a blanket, and Donner ripped his paw trying to escape. That's adaptable?"

"But when they saw you they melted."

"Apparently they melted for the soldier, too," I huffed.

"Don't be too hard on them," Ward cautioned. "They've gone through a lot recently—the shampoo, deworming pills, three days in a cage. Be thankful that they respond when someone—anyone—is nice to them. Lots of cats would sulk for days, but just look at them." He grinned and gestured toward the sofa.

Far from sulking, Donner and Tristan were play-wrestling like baby otters in a tug-of-war over a shabby catnip mouse. I smiled, but then had to choke back a sudden sob—the mouse had triggered a memory of Trushkie. With a sharp pang, I remembered how she had grinned and challenged us to endless games of Retrieve The Mouse. Though it was almost a year since

Trushkie's death, I was amazed at how often I still was choked up by sudden recollections of that precious kitten.

I shook my head to clear it and turned to an upcoming problem: In three weeks we were going to Munich for a week's vacation. What to do with the kittens? Obviously the clinic was out of the question.

The problem was solved a few days later when we mentioned it to our neighbors, Greg and Sue Randolf, over a game of bridge.

"They can stay with us!" Sue exclaimed. "We love the little dears."

We accepted the offer in a heartbeat although I beat down a twinge of guilt when I purposely neglected to warn them that they might be in for a week of steady howling.

Munich was marvelous, but on the long drive home our thoughts turned with anxiety to the kittens. How had they fared? Would Sue and Greg still be our friends even after we'd foisted two screaming kittens on them for a week? The more we talked about Donner and Tristan, the more eager I was to hold them. I found myself grinning idiotically at the thought that they'd soon be caressing my ankles and mewing with happiness. With growing impatience, I watched the long miles roll slowly by.

The minute we arrived in Bremerhaven, we went to the Randolf's. Outside their door, we paused to listen for howling, but all was quiet. "They're probably worn out," I whispered.

When Sue answered our knock, the scene that greeted us was a Norman Rockwell painting. Sue was in a flowered apron, the apartment was heady with the warm aroma of freshly baked chocolate chip cookies, Greg was slouched in an easy chair, grinning at the antics of our tiny twosome who were roughhousing in and out of a big, crinkly paper sack—far too absorbed in stalking and pouncing on one another to notice us.

Ward's eyebrows arched. His puzzled glance asked, "Are these the same kittens who almost knocked you over in their joy to see you?"

I shrugged, baffled—and a bit chargined. I knelt. "Hey, kitties, don't you know us?" I called.

Donner stopped in mid-pounce and spun in our direction. Tristan, with a little squeak of surprise, popped his head out of the bag to peer our way. For a fraction of a second they were startled into immobility. Then recognition flashed in their eyes and, in their traditional follow-the-leader fashion, they trotted—not ran—toward us, ears pricked and alert, tails high. Although they nuzzled and butted our outstretched hands, I sensed that their manner was somewhat aloof.

Well, of course we know you! We were a bit busy, that's all, they chattered in a strident Siamese greeting. Despite their friendly nuzzling, their tone clearly informed us that if we could leave them to go on vacation, then it was their feline right to assert their independence.

Stung by remorse, I scooped them up for a kiss and turned to Sue. "I hope they didn't howl too much," I said somewhat sheepishly.

"Howl?" she echoed. "Goodness, no. At first they explored the apartment. Sniffed in every corner. They obviously gave it their stamp of approval because within ten minutes they settled down in Greg's lap and purred to beat the band."

"Oh? They did?" I choked out weakly.

"They're adaptable little tykes," Greg added. "Had a great week. Be glad to cat-sit anytime."

I noticed, almost with regret, that the kittens' new security blanket had no holes. So—no howling, no chomping on wool. They must have felt right at home. I should have been thankful. Well, of course I was, I admonished myself. Wasn't I? But I was also... what? Disappointed? Yes. And jealous. *Face it, Barbara*, I scolded myself, *you're jealous because the kittens like everybody—not just you and Ward.*

As if they knew how hurt I was about their rompin' an' stompin' happily with the Randolfs, for the next few days Donner and Tristan had a complete change of heart. They clung to me like Velcro. They slept so close to my face that I could barely breathe. They followed my every move around the apartment, walking *directly* behind me. Like a parade of ducklings, we padded from room to room—me first, then Donner, his nose at my ankles, and Tristan trotting devotedly in the rear.

About that time, both Ward and I noticed that Tristan seemed especially devoted to me. Maybe his "second cat" status made him more attuned and sensitive to the fact that my feelings had been hurt by their affection for the young soldier and for the Randolfs.

Whatever the reason, every time I sat down, Tristan was emboldened to slyly push Donner from his choice position in the middle of my lap. Oh, he was crafty about it! He'd wait until Donner was snuggled down, purring, eyes at half-mast, too drowsy to be roused to action. Then Tristan would vault lightly to the top of the sofa just inches from my neck. There he would pause and casually lick his chest as if he had nothing else in the world to do. Then, slowly inching his front paws down the slope of the sofa, his body pressed as tightly as a magnet against mine, he would begin his gradual glide downward toward my lap. He slid stealthily, sinuously. When he reached lap level, with astonishing persistence and strength, slowly he elbowed Donner aside, artfully worming his way to the prime spot. Once or twice, annoyed at having his sleep disturbed, Donner flicked his paw at the intruder, but, with true grit, Tristan stayed his course and settled in, to purr, to nuzzle my hand, and to gaze up into my eyes as if to assure me that, of course, I held first place in his heart. *Don't get all in a snit about the Randolfs. Forgive us for upsetting you. After all, this is our home sweet home*, his manner seemed to say.

Of course, I forgave them. How could I not? I didn't know it then, but one day in the not-too-distant future, our cozy little world would be suddenly disrupted, and we would be always grateful for the kittens' friendship with the Randolfs.

Eleven

The Amazing "Comeback" Cats

I wish that I didn't have to write this chapter. I'm not proud of what I must say. I considered leaving it out, but if I did, the kittens' story would not be complete. Moreover, I hope that cat owners who face the problem we faced may benefit from our experience.

That problem was, the kittens were clawing our furniture to shreds.

Well, why not? Our sofa, courtesy of the U.S. Army Quartermaster Corps, was upholstered with a solid, thick, knobby fabric that cried out to be scratched and clawed. To the wide-eyed kittens the sofa looked like the world's biggest scratching post—a *Guiness Book of Records* post! Their look of joy said it all: *Wonder of wonders! A scratching post big enough for a battalion of cats! Surely, in coming to live with this generous couple we have entered kitten heaven.*

At first, Ward and I smiled and admired the kittens' grace when, as lithe as ballet dancers, they sashayed up to the sofa, stood on their hind legs, and reached up as high as possible on the armrests. The pose lengthened their backs and stretched them into a long, sinuous curve. With their front paws, they pulled and kneaded the textured material. Sometimes they moved as if in a trance, their eyes at half-mast with drunken delight. Their languid gestures were hypnotic. Other times, their imaginations wildly flashing, they attacked the armrests with sharp, quick stabs, growls, and fierce looks. *We are sworn to conquer this sofa!*

Charmed, we actually cheered them on, never thinking that those tiny paws would eventually slash and shred the upholstery until the tattered sofa looked like a molting buffalo.

When the first loose threads appeared, I clipped them with a nail scissors. Why, the damage was barely noticeable! But daily there were more and more loose threads. Before long, the upholstery became so threadbare that in spots the sofa's wooden frame peeked through the thin material.

We were no longer charmed by the supple stretches of the kittens. Now we worried about facing the Sergeant from the Quartermaster Corps. Scowling and muttering about the proper care of government property, he had charged us $18 for the khaki blanket that the kittens had chewed to Swiss cheese. Eighteen dollars for one blanket! What would he charge for destroying a sofa? One hundred dollars? Two hundred?

And even if we paid to replace it, the kittens would attack and demolish the new one, too.

Ward ordered a scratching post from the Post Exchange. It took two weeks to arrive, two weeks in which we shouted "No!" whenever a kitten even glanced toward the sofa, two weeks of continual thread clipping, two weeks of frustration, worry, and constant scoldings. The kittens sensed the change in our mood. Instead of running joyously to us for tummy rubbing and chin scratching, they approached us warily as if to ask, *What's going on? Is something wrong?* for despite our shouts of "No!" they seemed unaware that the sofa was not there specifically for their scratching pleasure.

"How can two smart kittens be so stupid?" I wailed.

Ward gave a grim laugh. "Stupid! Far from it. Plain old disobedience is more like it."

The scratching post finally arrived—a fine-looking post, upholstered with beige plush. We plunked it down next to the sofa. The curious kittens sidled up to it. They sniffed and circled, checking out every inch. They seemed intrigued. We waited, with held breath, for them to sink their claws into the plush pile. Instead, as if on command, they turned, and, in tandem they launched a ferocious attack on the sofa. I could swear that, as he slashed the armrest, Donner threw a disdainful glance over his shoulder at me. *You expect us to scratch on that puny little thing! Surely, you jest!*

We turned for advice to The Book. "Rub the scratching post with catnip and sprinkle white pepper on the sofa," it said.

Donner was the first to approach the catnip-scented post, but after the scantiest of sniffs, he shrugged his shoulders and turned away. *How boring.* Tristan followed suit. Clearly the meager whiff of catnip on the post was no match for the pungent batch of fresh catnip mice, gifts from my parents, which Tristan and Donner had stashed under the sofa, to be stalked and pounced upon at leisure. As for the pepper, they actually seemed to like the big, sloppy, head-clearing sneezes it brought on. Their eyes glinted with sly delight like snuff-sniffers in a Victorian novel.

Back to The Book.

"When you catch the cat scratching the furniture, snap out "No!" in sharp tones and immediately spritz the cat with water from a spray bottle," we read. "After three or four times, the cat will stop his inappropriate behavior."

I tried the new technique that afternoon. "NO!" I snapped sharply and, shooting from the hip with John Wayne speed and accuracy, I spritzed the kittens in mid-scratch.

It worked! Startled, they scurried out of range. Then, as if to hide their embarrassment at this undignified rebuke, they began to lick themselves with dedicated concentration as if a long bath had been on their afternoon agenda all along.

After that spritzing, we never again caught the kittens in the act. Yet, every morning the sofa was more shaggy. Obviously they were doing their dirty work in the dead of night. Locking them out of the living room did no good for they tortured us with their raucous Siamese shrieks until we raced to open the door.

Finally, I put into words the thought that had been lurking in the back of our minds. I took a deep breath. "Have you thought about... declawing?" I stammered.

Ward took a long time to answer. "Yes," he admitted. "I hate the idea, but I don't see how we can go on like this. It's not just the money, though that's bad enough, but this constant battling and shouting and tension is driving me up the wall."

Now that the subject was out in the open, it became an option to be considered. It was not a decision to be made lightly. We agonized. We talked late into the night and pored over The Book. To our surprise and dismay, The Book devoted only two short paragraphs to the subject. Declawing should be a last resort, it said, for it wasn't natural for a cat not to have claws. It stressed that a declawed cat *must* be kept indoors for it would have no way of defending itself against dogs, wild animals, or even other cats. We brushed that problem aside: Our cats were strictly indoor cats.

The next paragraph offered a shred of optimism: "Declawing does not cause psychological damage or behavioral problems nor does it affect a cat's ability to leap and balance." In our desperation to rationalize declawing, we focused on these words. If the kittens' personalities would not be affected, and if they'd still be able to run and leap, could declawing be all that bad?

However, when we consulted Dr. Armmand, he was furious that we'd even think of declawing. "Keep trying to get them used to the scratching post," he said. "Get a sturdier one. And, if worse comes to worst, let the cats claw the sofa. Live with it. Pay for the damage when you move. It's a small price for letting those kittens keep their only means of protection."

Before we had a chance to utter a word, he went on sternly. "And don't tell me that they're strictly house cats. I've heard that too many times. The truth is, that one day, they'll slip out of an open door and will be at the mercy of whatever attacks them.

"If you decide to go ahead with this, I will not do the operation," he added in an ominous tone. "You'll have to find a local vet."

We left his office, heavy with guilt and shame. We agreed to try a larger scratching post—if we could find one. But the instant we walked in the apartment and found both kittens industriously shredding the sofa, our good intentions dissolved. We exchanged a desperate look. Without a word, we both knew that it was time to find a German vet who would perform the operation.

At the risk of sounding as if I'm excusing our actions, I must say that our knowledge of declawing was vague. Both The Book and Dr. Armmand had focused on the kittens' loss of self-protection. Neither of them had described the declawing operation in its gory details. I wish they had, for in my ignorance, I imagined it as a form of clipping the kittens' nails—down to the quick, perhaps, which is painful enough, but I have since learned the brutal truth—declawing involves not only the nails, but, in fact, the tips of a cat's toes, including the bones, are amputated. Chopped off. It's a barbaric, excruciatingly painful mutilation of a living creature. (I have also learned that some experts believe that declawing can cause psychological problems.)

As if the declawing were not bad enough, on the advice of the German veterinarian who was recommended by German friends, we agreed to have the kittens neutered at the same time, to avoid anesthetizing them twice.

I'm amazed that I didn't smash up the car the morning I drove Donner and Tristan to the vet's, for my heart was pumping so hard that I actually thought it might explode, my head pounded with a tension headache, and my eyesight was a complete blur from welling tears.

Sensing that something bad was about to happen, the kittens cowered in fearful silence in the far corner of the carrying case. All I could see in the dimness were their wide, terrified eyes. Their occasional tiny, plaintive mews were nerve-wracking.

But the kittens were not my only concern. Ward was on my mind as well. The day before he had had an hour-and-a-half-long operation to extract an impacted wisdom tooth. I had left him in bed, moaning and clutching an ice-pack to his jaw, which had swollen to twice its normal size.

I was relieved to find that Dr. Schluter was a kindly, English-speaking man with a bright, clean clinic, but I

was nonplussed when he asked me to stay with the kittens to soothe them while he injected the anesthesia.

I reeled from the shock of watching it take effect
on Donner. He began to loll drunkenly and to retch
and heave before finally going limp. Instantly, an image of Trushkie on the operating table flashed through
my mind. On rubbery legs I crept to the waiting room
and sobbed.

It seemed ages before Dr. Schluter brought out the
kittens in the towel-lined basket I had brought for
them. Another rush of tears flooded my cheeks when I
saw them lying side by side—so tiny, still befuddled
and barely moving. It was one of the most pathetic
sights I'd ever seen. They looked so very vulnerable
and tender. And then, an obscenity to my eyes, I saw
that their front paws were encased in large gauze bandages, like boxing gloves, with traces of blood soaking
through. I think that was my first inkling of the true
horrors of declawing.

"That's normal. They're fine. Still a little groggy
from the anesthetic," Dr. Schluter assured me. "Don't
let them move around too much. And make sure the
bandages stay on. They'll try to gnaw them off."

I barely remember the drive home. My body was
drained and exhausted from stress. My limbs were limp
with relief that the kittens had survived, but the muscles
of my jaw and neck were rigid in sympathy for all the
pain surrounding me—the kittens' and Ward's.

And every time that I glanced down at the bloody
gauze bandages on the ends of the kittens' dear little

legs, my conscience felt the first terrible pangs of the guilt that have stayed with me all these years.

Back home, although Ward's swollen jaw still throbbed, he had improved enough to move from the bed to the sofa. The sight of the kittens shocked him. He was as surprised as I that the doctor had released them while they were still so groggy. We weren't prepared, emotionally or practically, to cope with such limp, weak forms and gauzy wads of blood-smudged bandages. I set the basket near the sofa, piled cushions on the floor next to it and collapsed on them. Worn, spent, and worried, we began an all-night vigil.

As the kittens came around, groggy and bewildered, their eyelids opened slowly, drowsily, as if burdened by sleep.

"Donner. Tristan," I murmured over and over. "You're all right, little ones. We're here. We're here." Donner stirred as if trying to sit up. Ward and I exchanged a hopeful glance, but immediately we winced, for as consciousness returned, so did pain. Donner's pitiful mew was the saddest sound I had ever heard. Moments later, Tristan, trying to rise, was also knocked back by the knife-like pain. Ward sucked in his breath sharply, and a dreadful shiver ran up and down my arms.

However, there wasn't time for self-rebuke, for at that moment, the kittens saw one another—and the basket seemed to explode with sudden fury. The kittens' ears went flat back, their eyes narrowed, and in a frenzy of fear, hate, and pain, they tried to pull themselves up to attack one another, all the while snarling, hissing, and spitting. I had no idea that they could turn into such raging animals. Wearing potholder mittens, I managed to put them in separate towel-lined boxes, then made a frantic call to Dr. Schluter.

"I should have warned you," he apologized. "The kittens don't recognize one another because they smell of medicine. They'll be fine when it wears off. Meantime, keep them apart."

I'll never forget that night. Within an hour, both kittens, working furiously with their teeth, chewed off their bandages. Dazed and clearly in pain, they tried to lick the blood from their wounds. It was a nerve-wracking struggle to hold them, sprinkle their paws with penicillin powder, and wrap them with clean gauze without pressuring their tender toes. In no time, the kittens chewed off our loose, makeshift bandages, and soon we were out of gauze. By now I was in tears, and Ward's jaw pulsed with pain as he staggered around from neighbor to neighbor to borrow tape and bandages.

By daybreak, we had changed the dressings four times. The living room was an arena of soiled bandages, spilled powder, scraps of gauze, and the four of us were sprawled, exhausted, and limp, like battle casualties.

It took two days for the medicinal odor to wear off. That morning, miraculously, the kittens awakened, stretched luxuriously, limped toward one another and, as if nothing extraordinary had happened, took turns grooming one another's ears and faces. They still hobbled on tender, bandaged paws, but surely they were recovering. Again I cried—from sheer relief.

Ward also recuperated. His sutures were removed. His pain diminished. I knew that he was back to his old self when he wanted me to gaze in awe and wonder at the size of the hole in his jaw.

It was over a week before Donner and Tristan were once again frisking around the apartment, and although there weren't any apparent physical or psychological ill-effects from the declawing, I harbored guilt that remains to this day. At the time, however, we were grateful that the affair had ended well. Now Christmas was coming. We turned our thoughts to the upcoming holidays.

Visions danced in my head—not visions of sugarplums but enticing visions of cozy, snowy evenings, of hot, mulled cider, lovely carols, and two, blissful kittens curled among gift-wrapped packages under a garland-draped Christmas tree—visions as warm and fuzzy as a Norman Rockwell Christmas card.

When I drew a verbal image of this peaceful vision to Ward, he glanced with wry amusement at the kittens who, at the moment, were rioting through the living room, growling like hungry lions and tossing and mauling a tattered, catnip mouse. Ward gave me a raised-eyebrow look as if he'd had a glimpse of the coming holidays—and Norman Rockwell was nowhere in sight.

"Dream on," he said with a sly smile. "Dream on."

It turned out that Ward, like the prophets of old, knew whereof he spoke.

Twelve

Masters Of
The Art Of Escape

Something strange was going on: Donner and Tristan kept escaping, Houdini-like, from locked rooms.

The mystery began when we decorated the Christmas tree. The cats thought that they'd entered cat heaven. Right there, in their own living room, was the biggest cat toy they'd ever seen! All those dangling balls to knock down, wallop, and whack around! So much sparkling, swaying, tinsel to bat at! So many shimmery bows to be chewed and tattered. The gleam in their eyes as they frolicked around the tree said it all: *Joy to the world! Isn't Christmas the greatest? Does life get any better than this?*

We were charmed by their enthusiasm, and as long as they didn't climb the tree, we had a liberal play policy—except, of course, when we went out. Then we herded them out of the living room and closed the door to protect both Donner and Tristan and the tree.

At least that was our intent. But every time we came home we found the cats romping around the living room in rowdy games of kick-ball with ornaments they'd swatted off the fir branches.

At first, Ward and I accused one another of leaving the door ajar. But even when we double-checked the door before leaving, the cats were partying in the living room when we returned. Baffling. And worrying. Two cats plus one Christmas tree could add up to trouble.

And, sure enough, one day there *was* trouble—almost tragedy. We came home to find the tree on its side, slivers of broken glass ornaments glittering across the carpet, and Donner hunkered down in the debris. At first, I thought he was stalking a tiny angel ornament, but when I looked more closely, I was struck with horror for Donner's eyes were squeezed shut, his body shuddered, and a fearful rasp broke from his throat. He was choking on a strand of tinsel. Five inches of the shimmery "icicle" hung from his mouth. He was working his tongue back and forth to get rid of it, but with each horrible gag, the tinsel inched farther down his throat.

For a moment we froze remembering The Book's dire warning about not letting cats swallow strings or thread; they could become entangled internally and cause great suffering and even death. I also remembered—the words were seared into my brain—that it is dangerous to pull a string from a cat's mouth because his tongue is covered with hundreds of tiny, hooked projections. This roughness is an aid to grooming, but it also makes it difficult to pull out a string. In fact, it may cause the string to break in the animal's throat.

Panic-stricken, our thoughts racing, we knelt beside Donner. It would take at least 15 minutes to rush him to the vet. He could choke to death in that time. Something had to be done—*quickly*.

Instinctively, I reached for the tinsel with shaky fingers. I gave a gentle, tentative tug.

"What do you think? Will it come out?" Ward's whisper was low and urgent.

I licked my lips and gave a terse nod. "I think it gave way a little. I'll try. I have to," I whispered back.

Ward stood. "I'll get the vet on the line." His voice was tight.

I tried to stroke and calm Donner as much as possible. But he was choking too much to be comforted. Once again, with held breath, I grasped the tinsel. My mouth was bone-dry, but I began to sweat as *slowly, slowly*, I pulled on the delicate strand. How fragile it felt! A mere shimmering wisp—so beautiful, but so dangerous. "Please, God, don't let it break off in Donner's throat," I prayed. "And please don't let it cut his tender tissues."

By fractions of an inch, with each tiny, quivering tug, the slippery strand began to emerge. It was mesmerizing to watch it grow. The tension in the room was almost palpable. Ward, totally rapt, didn't realize that his finger had stopped in mid-dial.

After what seemed endless time, the last bit of tinsel slipped from Donner's tongue. He stopped gagging and opened his eyes. We had it—all of it!

I slumped back on my heels, exhausted. Ward collapsed beside me, both of us slack-limbed as the tension drained away. We stared at the strand of limp, wet tinsel. Later we measured it. It was 18 inches long! It was a miracle that it had not broken.

Then we both stared in astonishment. Next to us, as if nothing had happened, Donner was calmly grooming himself. He seemed so content we wouldn't have been surprised if he'd started to hum a cheerful tune.

"It's amazing," I exclaimed. "Animals have no concept of their own death. Donner has no idea how close he came to dying."

Just then, out of the corner of my eye. I caught a movement. It was Tristan. During the tense moments he had huddled off to one side, silently staring with wide, puzzled eyes. Now he crept forward, his belly grazing the floor, his elongated neck extended toward Donner. Sniffing, he slunk closer and closer. Then, tentatively at first, but soon with deliberate care, he began to lick his friend's face and ears. Donner's eyes closed in rapture.

"Well, back to normal," Ward grinned as we cleaned the mess and meticulously plucked every strand of tinsel from the tree. "Except we still don't know how they get into the living room!"

But I had a plan. The next morning, realizing that I might be in for a long siege, I armed myself with a book and a thermos of coffee and sequestered myself with the cats in the small hallway that separated the back of our apartment from the front. I closed the door that led to the living room. I closed it securely. I double-checked it. It was firm. Tight. I sat on the floor and took up my book, determined to stay with the cats until I discovered their secret.

"Okay, guys. Let's see you get out," I challenged.

In answer they sat like little sentinels squarely before me and, with charmingly cocked heads, gazed expectantly into my eyes. The pose was beguiling— I'd swear they'd been practicing it. *You closed the door. You open it*, it implied.

"Sorry," I said and pretended to read.

A half-hour passed. The cats remained like statues except for their longing gazes, which were so pitiful that I almost gave in.

Finally, Donner moved. He rose, arched his back in a lazy stretch, then sat down in front of the door… and cried. Oh, what a pleading little mew, intended to break my heart. When I continued to read, his heart-rending pleas grew louder… and louder… and louder… until they ballooned into ear-shattering screams that demanded attention. Between cries, Donner glanced my way. His querying look asked, *Well, had enough? Ready to give in?*

When I ignored him, he turned to Tristan with a look of scorn. *You could help, you know.* Tristan got the message, sidled up to Donner, and now their combined chorus of shrieks bounced and echoed off the walls of the tiny space. My eardrums vibrated, but I remained firm.

For their next ploy, the cats combined cuteness with direct action. Lowering their heads, with a gesture they knew to be absolutely adorable, they repeatedly butted my hands. Usually this was an urgent request for a scratch behind the ears. But not this time. This time the head-butting was meant to chide me, to force me to close my book! *We are too cute to ignore. Put down that silly novel and open the door!*

"Sorry," I repeated and buried my nose in the pages.

Fifteen minutes later, Donner gave up on me. He strutted to the door. With one final exasperated glance at me, he stood on his hind legs and stretched as high as possible toward the door handle. Instead of a knob, the handle was a horizontal lever about six inches long. It was about three inches above Donner's longest reach. I thought that he might yowl again for help, but that three-inch gap didn't frustrate him in the least. Instead, he went into a semi-crouch, bunched his muscles, and jumped. And missed. And jumped again. And again.

My mouth was agape at Donner's persistence. Even if he could reach the handle, what good would it do? The handle was smooth and clean-lined, and Donner had no claws. I shook my head. "You're a kooky little cat, Donner," I muttered.

But then, on Donner's sixth jump, his paws grabbed the handle and curled tenaciously around it—without claws! For a frozen moment he hung there, securing his grip. Then, with unbelievable balance and skill, he began to inch backward, sliding his curled paws toward the end of the lever! It was an amazing feat. I watched with wonder. Tristan, on the other hand, took it in with an off-hand air. *I've seen him do this a dozen times*, his manner said—which, of course, he had!

When Donner's paws reached the end of the lever, the weight of his body brought the lever down. With a solid click, the door opened. Donner dropped down lightly. Shooting a *How about that?* look at me, with a bold swagger, he led Tristan into the living room, straight to the tree. Then, with the casual, confident stroke of a tennis ace, he swung at the ornaments until one fell. *Look sharp!* he snapped at Tristan and swatted the glittering ball his way.

Tristan proved equally athletic. He pounced and batted the ball back and forth between swift paws with the dash and daring of a soccer star.

I was left sitting there, dazed, amazed, amused, and, in spite of myself, cheering and applauding like a crazed soccer fan.

Thirteen

The Cuckoo Clock Caper

As the months passed, Donner and Tristan slowly grew from cuddly, clownish little critters with over-sized paws, into graceful adult cats. We were constantly awed by their beauty, whether they were stretching luxuriously in a patch of sun, curling up in the snug hollow of a sofa cushion, or stalking catnip mice with silent, sinuous grace.

Tristan's fur, so pale when he was a kitten, deep-ened to an egg-shell shade, with a dusting of fawn color on his back. His mask, ears, legs, feet, and tail gradu-ally turned dark brown. His finely sculpted, triangu-lar-shaped head was in perfect proportion to his el-egant neck and long-limbed body. His blue eyes, slightly slanted, enhanced his lean look. We had no idea of how he would rank in a cat show, but in our judgment he was flawless. I only wished that he would get over his "second cat" mentality, for, in spite of his beauty, which should have given him lordly confidence, Tristan still deferred to Donner. He still walked a half pace behind and still gazed with pride, like a worshipful little brother, at Donner's "top cat" accomplishments.

"Assert yourself just a little bit, Tristan," I constantly urged him. But he seemed content in Donner's shadow.

Because we loved Donner so dearly, in our eyes, he was a most handsome fellow, but, I suspect, he would have been "shown the door" at a cat show. His head was still more round than triangular, and his eyes were a tad crossed. This gave him a somewhat forlorn look which was endearing to us, but would not win points in a cat show. Moreover, his overall chocolate color was too dark for consideration as a prize-winning Siamese, although we thought it was gorgeous and loved to bury our noses in it when Donner snuggled under our chins.

Donner didn't give a hoot about his imperfections—if he was even aware of them. In fact, he had an extraordinarily high opinion of himself. He was confident that he could do anything he chose to do, and his door handle trick only added to his cockiness. Pride gleamed from those slightly crossed eyes and was apparent in every movement of his agile, firmly muscled body. The cat definitely had *attitude*. Donner didn't walk—he strutted. Ears upright and alert, he carried his head high, at a rakish angle. His tail stood straight up as if he were on military parade—the epitome of a jaunty cat who intended to be noticed.

But then, one night, the mighty was laid low. Donner was taken down a peg or two by, of all things, a tiny bird—the wooden bird in our new cuckoo clock! The bird was boisterous and every bit as jaunty as Donner. Every half hour he popped out to announce the passing of time. He discharged this duty with great dash. On the hour, he was accompanied by schmaltzy renditions of *Tales Of The Vienna Woods*. On the half hour, he performed to the lilting strains of *The Blue Danube*. Donner became obsessed with this warbler. We suspected that he realized that the cuckoo's cockiness might match—or even surpass—his own. This would not do. A showdown seemed inevitable.

The build-up to the confrontation between Donner and the saucy cuckoo began on the cuckoo's first day in the house. It was my birthday, and Ward had given me the clock as a gift as we celebrated in a quaint German restaurant, toasting with more champagne than necessary before frolicking home at midnight to hang the clock.

Awakened by our spirited activity, Donner and Tristan rubbed the sleep from their eyes and shuffled in to the kitchen. They eyed us suspiciously. *Why were these merry-makers up so late, and what was that wooden object they were hanging next to the refrigerator? And why so much hammering? Good grief, a cat can't get a decent night's sleep.*

"Look, kitties, a bird!" Ward cried. He swept the clock hands to twelve o'clock. Out popped the bird, chest puffed, cuckooing mightily.

Both cats instantly froze, then, slowly, slowly, they lowered their haunches to a pounce position and focused their laser-beam eyes on the tantalizing bird high above them. Their jaws chattered in a tooth-rattling staccato as if they were already munching the juicy morsel. Then, like mini-rockets, they launched themselves upward. But the clock was too high. They tumbled back down, just as the cuckoo ducked inside.

Hey! The cats scrambled to their feet. Whiskers stiffened. Muzzles twitched. Puzzled, they stared at where the bird had been. I giggled. Donner turned and shot me an accusing glance. *I suspect you're behind this*, he glowered, then again riveted his eyes on the clock.

Still bubbly gay from the champagne, we teased the poor cats by advancing the clock hands swiftly in half-hour increments, making the bird appear and disappear in a frenzy of cuckooing. The cats went wild. Whipped to a frenzy, they forsook stealth. Instead, they made repeated scrambling attacks up the wall, but each time they fell back in ignominious heaps.

Finally, Donner fired a furious look at us and flounced off, grumbling, to the living room. Tristan sashayed behind him. Feigning a great pretense of having forgotten the stupid bird, they began to bathe with intense concentration. They fooled no one. Hatred of that bird was imprinted on their brains, and twice, that night, we were awakened by sounds of cats' bodies leaping and falling, leaping and falling.

The next morning, Donner decided to tackle the problem from a different angle. I swear I heard him exclaim *Ah ha!* as he studied the situation and suddenly realized that he might get to the bird if he jumped from the floor to a chair, to the counter and, finally, to the top of the fridge. *Now, why didn't I think of that before?* he sputtered, and I could practically see him smack his forehead with his paw. In three graceful bounds he was atop the fridge, his eyes glowing with victory.

But his celebration was brief, for Donner had not reckoned with our large breadbox. Tucked beneath the overhanging cabinets, it took up most of the top of the fridge. Donner had just enough space to perch in one corner. Although this "can do" cat was only two feet from the clock, the breadbox was an immovable obstacle that barred him from reaching it.

As if the bird knew that he was home free, he hopped out and warbled as lustily as if he were auditioning to be a cuckoo in Big Ben. Clutching the edges of the fridge, Donner stretched his neck and leaned as far around the breadbox as he could. His climbing and clinging skills were worthy of a Nepalese sherpa, but not quite good enough to conquer the breadbox. Chattering his teeth in a frenzy of frustration, he shot daggers at the small songster.

At that point, something was triggered in Tristan who was watching, with head cocked, eyes narrowed in concentration. What suddenly possessed him to crash the scene, I'll never know, but with a squeak of joy and adventure he leaped—chair, counter top, top of fri… Ooops! The realization came in a flash—there was no room up there! For a frantic moment, Tristan clung to the slippery edge of the fridge with his front paws while his hind legs scrabbled for traction on its slick side. Then, with a startled squeak, he crashed to the floor. Unhurt but ruffled and embarrassed, he glowered at me, daring me to laugh. Then he slunk off, muttering darkly about a certain stupid, German cuckoo.

Nor did Donner ever catch that cocky, teasing bird. At first we worried about his pride. Was it irrevocably wounded? After all, the bird was one-twentieth Donner's size. Would Donner lose his swagger? His cockiness?

Worry about Donner's pride? Ha! We should have known better. Whenever Donner was handed a lemon, he made lemonade. This time his "lemonade" was a king-of-the-hill perch atop the fridge from which to oversee all kitchen activity. His nonchalance said it all: *Who cares about that silly bird, anyway?*

I marveled at how quickly Donner shifted gears. From the miserable, hunched position of a defeated hunter, he now rose to a stately, seated pose next to the breadbox. As if sitting for his portrait by Rembrandt, he planted his front legs as straight and slim as columns, his tail neatly coiled around his paws. He squared his shoulders and held his head grand, high, and serene. Without knowing it—or did he?—Donner had assumed the imperial stance of the cat goddess statutes of ancient Egypt.

From then on, every evening, Donner leaped to his high roost to supervise dinner preparations. Not once did he condescend to glance at the cuckoo.

As for Tristan, he pointedly ignored Donner when he was perched atop the fridge. Why should he hang around under Donner's proud nose at the scene of his embarrassing leap and clumsy fall? Instead, he turned on his heel and, with stately tread, strolled away. *Who needs it?* his manner implied.

"That's the way to go, Tristan!" I exclaimed at this rare show of assertiveness. Tristan grinned slyly as if the two of us were punching up a "high five."

As the months passed, the four of us became a close-knit family with typical family joys and squabbles, adjusting gradually, with good humor, to each other's personalities and peculiarities. Our occasional illnesses had deepened our bonds even further. For instance, if Donner and Tristan caught a cold, at their slightest sniffle, we were immediately flooded with memories of *Neunzig's* fatal illness, and we anxiously checked on them several times both day and night.

On the other hand, when a tension headache sent me to bed in a darkened room, both cats leaped up to snuggle at my side as if they instinctively knew that their quiet presence and the warmth of their gently pulsing bodies had a powerful calming effect.

By sharing both good times and bad with Donner and Tristan, we began to truly understand the pure love, joy, and the sense of belonging to one another that is possible between humans and cats.

However, this tranquil, domestic scene was about to end. Six months later, Ward burst in one day with news that shattered our snug little family. Quite unexpectedly, he had received a set of orders. In exactly one month we were to leave for his new duty station in Washington, D.C., 14 months earlier than originally scheduled. To complicate matters, the orders included attendance at two naval intelligence schools en route to Washington.

Our emotions were ragged. We were thrilled and excited about the speciality training, which would enhance Ward's career, but we were also distraught because we'd be "on the road," in and out of motels and temporary quarters, for four months. We had to face the major question of what to do with Donner and Tristan.

It's strange how you sometimes recall certain events with incredible clarity. I can visualize the day that Ward came home with his news. I was making macaroni and cheese. Donner, atop the fridge, was leaning precariously over to tap my shoulder with an outstretched paw, a subtle reminder that he was in need of a bit of cheese. Tristan, in the doorway, was begging for his share with tiny mews and irresistible, woeful looks.

At Ward's surprise announcement, my first reaction was disappointment. There were still so many places in Europe left to visit! Then I remembered the cats. My God! Could we uproot them and drag them around in a vagabond lifestyle for four months? It was totally impractical. My mind raced. I wondered if our parents could keep them until we got settled in Washington.

Ward had already considered this. "No way," he said. "Your mother is uneasy around cats, and my parents have Jamie."

I sighed, recalling how my mother froze when a cat came near her, and I definitely remembered Jamie, the very large, very anti-cat dog who ruled Ward's parents' home.

All through dinner, which we barely touched, and on into the night, we mulled over the problem until we were exhausted and irritable. We explored every possible way to take Donner and Tristan with us, but the obstacles were overwhelming—months on the road, moving in and out of motels and Navy transient housing. At midnight, we finally accepted the dismaying, inevitable fact—we had to find a home for the cats in Germany.

On a small military base, news travels with lightning speed. At the monthly Wives' Club luncheon the next day, I mentioned our problem, and, by dinner time, half the base knew about it. That evening, in the middle of dessert, Sue and Greg Randolf called. They had just heard the news, and they offered—pleaded—to take Donner and Tristan. As a civilian who worked for the Army, Greg had a less globe-trotting career than Ward. The Randolfs would be in Germany at least four more years.

"We love Donner and Tristan, and you know they got along fine with us before," Sue said. "So, this is the perfect solution—and I promise to care for them as lovingly as you do."

I was so choked with a rush of gratitude, relief, and sorrow all mixed up together that I could barely speak. Yes, I certainly did remember how quickly Donner and Tristan had taken to the Randolfs while we were on vacation. And I remembered how we had laughingly called them "The Little Traitors." Now I knew that

Sue was right. This was the perfect solution. With heartfelt, if sorrow-tinged, thanks, we agreed to give the cats to the Randolfs two days before our departure, so they'd be out of the apartment before the arrival of the packers and movers.

When I hung up, I was trembling. We had solved the problem, and though we were relieved, we weren't happy. Exhausted by our emotions, we gazed tiredly at the cats, who slept, blissfully innocent, in a snug hollow of a sofa cushion.

That month was bittersweet. We spoiled the cats shamelessly. When Donner begged for a tidbit of cheese, I gave him chunks of it. I knew it was wrong. Too much fat. But I wanted to give him the world. I wanted to give him my heart. I wanted him to remember me with love. It was the same with Tristan who was always there in his big brother's shadow, gazing patiently up at me. At the cats' slightest plea for a tummy rub, a chin scratch, or a game of chase-the-string, we dropped everything to do their bidding. On the sofa, in the evening, we hugged them to us so tightly that they squirmed away. We tried to imprint their image on our brains. Through eyes misty with tears, I watched Donner, high and regal, atop the fridge. I studied every inch of his sturdy frame, memorizing how he held his head, how he curled his tail. Admiring Tristan, sprawled on his back in the sunshine, I clicked his image in my mind, another snapshot for my mental photo album of memories. I wept easily in those last days, and Ward was uncharacteristically subdued. I often caught him gazing pensively at the cats.

On the final day, I envied Ward for having office work to take his mind off the cats. I should have been preparing for the packers. Instead, heavy-hearted and restless, I wandered around the apartment and tried to get the cats to snuggle with me one last time, but they sensed that something was wrong, and they shied away.

It was a somber little caravan that plodded to the Randolfs that evening. Ward toted Donner and Tristan in their carrier. I hauled a basket heaped with food dishes, litter, litter pan, and the cats' toy collection.

Although Sue and Greg were excited about adopting the cats, sensitive to our sadness, they welcomed us solemnly. When Ward knelt to open the door of the cats' carrier, it suddenly hit me that this was the moment we had to leave them, and I shuddered with a sudden sigh. My eyesight blurred as I watched the cats step from the carrier, cautiously at first, then boldly, as they recognized their surroundings.

Sue and Greg stood apart as we said our good-byes. Ward knelt, gathered both cats to him and stroked them the way they enjoyed it—firmly, with a cupped palm, down the full length of their bodies, from their foreheads to their arched spines to the tips of their raised tails. Such bliss! *Again*, they begged by butting their lowered heads against his hand, but Ward was too shaken. He rose and turned away, surreptitiously wiping his eyes.

I knelt and scooped up both cats and buried my face in their fur. "Good-bye, kitties," I whispered. "Be good. We'll never forget you." Tristan saw the tear that coursed down my cheek and, curious, batted at it. His gentle touch undid me. Tears streaming, I rose and let the cats leap lightly down—and that was the last time we touched one another.

During the next two days, Sue called several times to assure us that the cats were fine, but on the third day, the morning of our flight, I suddenly ached to see them one last time.

At the Randolf's, when no one answered my ring, I remembered that it was Sue's day to volunteer at the library. Dejected, I sagged against the doorjamb. Then I eyed the small, narrow window to the right of the door. It was against all my instincts to peer into someone's apartment, but, glancing around to make sure I was alone, I pressed my nose to the glass. By squinting through the sheer, lacy curtain, I could see— a limited, blurry view—into the living room. There, asleep on the sofa, were Donner and Tristan. I held my breath and stared at them until my eyes ached from squinting.

"Donner. Tristan." I found myself whispering their names over and over.

Finally, my sight blurred by tears, I slowly turned away.

Fourteen

We Are Adopted!

The scene was enchanting. In a cushioned wicker basket, a Siamese mother cat curled around a jumbled heap of plump, milk-white kittens snuggled close to her tummy.

I dropped to my knees and sighed. Four months had passed since my farewell glimpse of Donner and Tristan in Germany. Now, settled in the Washington, D.C. area, Ward and I were as excited as kids at the prospect of getting two kittens. A classified ad had brought us to this chic townhouse in affluent Georgetown, the home of Eloise Forrestert, a seal-point Siamese cat breeder. She turned out to be an attractive woman in designer jeans and silk shirt. Her "cat room"—a sunny, glass-enclosed porch—and her elegant appearance were in vivid contrast to the battered black satchel and ragamuffin wardrobe of *Frau* Schmidt.

Mrs. Forrestert had screened us over the phone, explaining her standards for prospective purchasers of her purebred kittens. These included a written promise that we would neuter the kittens, keep their shots up-to-date and raise them as "inside cats." Also, for the kittens' optimum physical and emotional health, Mrs. Forrestert refused to separate them from their mother until they were nine weeks old.

We vowed to abide by her rules and were invited to visit. There was no promise that we'd be allowed to buy—or, in her words, "to adopt"—a kitten. I sensed that we were still on trial.

"I'm surprised that she doesn't make us sign in blood," I remarked. Ward laughed, but, in fact, we were glad that she was careful. We still flinched at the memory of *Frau* Schmidt's grimy shop and the tragic fate of little *Neunzig*.

Now, kneeling beside me, Mrs. Forrestert scooped up a soft little ball and tucked it into my cupped hands. "This is number three, the third-born."

"You can tell them apart?"

"Goodness, yes. Every one is a distinct little personality. I call this one "Snooze.""

I could see why. Through half-closed lids, Snooze sized me up and signaled her trust by falling into a deep sleep. I sighed, so low that it was practically a purr. I had almost forgotten the pleasure of stroking a contented, utterly limp kitten.

Mrs. Forrestert settled a slumbering kitten in Ward's palm. "Sassy—the second-born," she whispered. Sassy instantly lived up to her name by opening her eyes, glaring at Ward and scolding him with tiny, indignant yelps at being awakened!

"Sorry, Sassy, sorry," Ward murmured and stroked her lightly under her chin. Ward's charm worked again; almost instantly Sassy's eyes softened in a gloppy look of affection.

With Snooze and Sassy cuddled under our chins, Ward and I grinned idiotically at one another.

Mrs. Forrestert smiled. I had a feeling that she approved of us. "I think you've found your kittens," she said.

At that moment we were distracted by a noise from the basket where the plumpest kitten in the heap was wriggling out from the jumble of legs, tails, and sleepy heads. With urgent squawks, he cried for us to wait. *Don't make a hasty decision… I'm coming… coming….*

In his haste, he toppled from the basket and landed head-down and rump-up. Undaunted, this little creature scrambled upright and continued his tiny, insistent entreaties. The words *confident, fearless, and adorable* sprang to my mind!

"That's Thor—Kitten Number One," Mrs. Forrestert laughed. "As you can see, a bold one."

My heart flipped as Thor padded toward us on ludicrously outsized paws, his pearl-pink triangle of a nose twitching in greeting and his whip-thin tail waving as proudly as a pennant on a sailboat. Releasing Snooze and Sassy—they toddled groggily back to Mama—we stretched our hands toward this feisty fellow.

To our surprise, instead of rushing to Ward for instant male bonding, the kitten headed my way. With what, I swear, was a flirtatious glance, he lowered his head, charged, butted my knee—and collapsed, off-balance in a clownish half-somersault.

I started to laugh, then caught myself, remembering how my laughter had once wounded Donner's pride when he had lost his balance while cavorting high atop a curtain rod. He had flailed frantically—comically, I thought—like a cartoon character, but Donner hadn't thought it was funny. When he recovered his footing, he strolled away with deliberate nonchalance, his chin high, the shreds of his dignity wrapped around him like a treasured old cloak. Chagrined, I never again laughed at his foibles.

Thor, on the other hand, took my laughter as a call for several encores of butting and tumbling. Finally, however, he rolled onto his back and stretched lazily—a coy invitation for me to stroke the snowy mound of his tummy!

I was thrilled by the vibrations of his purr, beginning as a light pulse under my fingertips, then swelling to a deep throb as Thor closed his eyes and stretched himself out, long and lean.

Just then Mrs. Forrestert pointed to the basket where a delicate but determined kitten was squirming out from under her dozing siblings. "It's Blossom, number six."

"Oh-h-h my!" I held my breath, enraptured, as the kitten, her body held low, glided warily toward us. So tiny and so slow moving, she blended almost perfectly into the thick pile of the light-colored carpet. Six inches from our fingertips she stopped, statue still. Slowly, slowly elongating her body, she stretched toward us. Her ears were pricked, her cornflower blue eyes big with curiosity and caution. At last her nose made feather-light contact with the tip of my finger. She sniffed, oh, so delicately! My skin tingled at her cool touch.

Then, just as slowly, she sank back, her taut limbs and wide eyes softening. With studied precision, she tucked her paws under her chest and artfully arranged her tail in a tight curl around her body. When she was precisely in place, a neat, trusting little package, she looked up at us and began to purr. A booming, startlingly loud purr from such a tiny creature!

I ached to scoop her up but sensed that for the time being she'd prefer being admired from afar. I also sensed that she could become a very affectionate kitten.

That was how we acquired Thor and Blossom. There was no debate, no agonizing decision. It simply happened. *They* adopted *us*.

The kittens were two days shy of nine weeks, but we coaxed Mrs. Forrestert to waive her nine-week rule. So they were ours, and we were theirs. And that was that.

We drove home with the kittens tucked into a towel-lined cardboard box. I left the box top askew so I could keep an eye on them. Ward leaned over and peered in at every stoplight.

"So, what'll we do about their names?" he asked. "You like "Thor" and "Blossom"?"

"Not especially, and I really want to name them ourselves, don't you?"

Ward nodded but sighed. We'd been thinking about names for weeks and hadn't come up with even one. We wanted names with an oriental sound, suitable for Siamese. We had considered, but rejected *Dok Rak* meaning "flower of love," *Chanthra* or "moon," *Sud* meaning "Tiger," and *Bun Mi*, "to have luck."

Then, as luck would have it, after all our pondering, within ten minutes the kittens virtually named themselves. Thor was first when, bracing his legs solidly, he rose to his full height—all of eight inches!—and raucously demanded to know why he was cooped up in this box. Didn't we realize that he was born to explore?

"Look at him! That defiant stance! Just like a sumo wrestler," Ward said. Since our short vacation in Japan a few years earlier, we were big fans of all things Japanese, including sumo wrestling and the reigning sumo champion, a robust giant called Taiho.

"You're right!" I said. "Want to call him "Taiho?" Perfect, isn't it?"

Ward gave it exactly a one-second thought, then grinned and nodded, for, incredible as it seemed, with his four-square bold stance, this cocky, 38-ounce kitten mimicked the posture of the 400-pound wrestler. So, "Taiho" it was. And not long after, it was "Tai," for short.

We studied little Blossom, curled in a corner with her chin nestled between her paws. She was so demure, so shy, and so utterly feminine. To us, she seemed the epitome of an oriental princess—and instantly we knew that she had to be "Michiko"—"Mikko," for short—the name of Japan's charming royal princess. Eventually she'd also be known as the less-elegant "Meeks" and "Squeako."

I could hardly believe how easy it had been. And so perfect. I leaned over the box and nuzzled the kittens.

"Hello, Taiho. Hello, Mikko," I whispered.

Mikko lightly licked the tip of my nose and gave me a gentle look.

"MEEEOOOWWW." Taiho's sumo-wrestler-size cry for attention shattered the peace of the moment. Far from minding it, we loved it. It was why we wanted to live with Siamese. We loved their constant chatter, their prattling, gossiping, bellowing, squawking, scolding, and muttering. We loved their gregariousness, their desire to be always involved in our lives. And these two promised to do just that.

Within minutes of arriving home, we realized that, once again, like Donner and Tristan, we had a "top cat" (Taiho, naturally) and a "second cat." The scenario began when I removed the box lid. With an impatient squawk, Taiho leaped out. He froze momentarily for, bold though he was, he was also cautious, because who knew what unseen dangers lurked in this strange place?

Mikko followed, a moment later, but because her leap was not as bold nor as mighty, she landed in a squeaking sprawl. At the sudden noise, Taiho went into full alert—spitting, hissing, arching his back, bristling his whiskers, spiking his fur, and springing sideways in stiff-legged hops. The transformation from gentle kitten to fierce feline was swift and astonishing.

We stared, amazed. Then, even more amazed, we gawked at Mikko who crouched motionless, her wide eyes fixed on Taiho and her head tilted submissively as if imploring forgiveness for having startled him.

When Taiho realized that there was no danger, the moment of suspense evaporated as quickly as it had started. Somewhat sheepishly, he lowered his rigid back, then casually licked a curled paw as if to remark, *Handled that rather neatly, I'd say*. When Mikko sidled up to him a moment later to tentatively lick him behind the ear, Taiho regarded the gesture as an apology, which, with a proud pose, he grandly accepted.

"Nicely done," Ward murmured.

"Hmmmm." I wasn't so sure. It struck me that Mikko was being awfully servile for such a minor "offense."

Ward grinned. He knew how I hated it when females—cats included—acted as if inferior to males. "I don't think Mikko knows about equal rights. You'll have to square her away," he whispered.

I jabbed him in the ribs. "I just might do that," I retorted.

Probably because of the loving care they had received at Mrs. Forrestert's, both kittens—especially

Taiho—were amazingly self-assured and unafraid. Eagerly they explored the house, stalking and attacking anything that moved—a fluttering curtain, swaying fringe, dangling lamp chain, even flickering, sunlit motes of dust. In the kitchen they stood on hind legs and craned their necks, in vain, to see the tops of the fridge and counter, but these were veritable Mount Everests, too slick for climbing, too high for leaping. As they turned away, Taiho's rueful glance back at us clearly promised that one day he would return as conqueror.

As the kittens' boldness grew, they scaled the backs of the sofa and easy chairs, their tiny claws scratching and snagging most satisfactorily in the deep weave. They ignored the brand new scratching post. "Lessons in the proper use of a scratching post will begin in the morning at seven," Ward informed them.

Watching the kittens explore, I thought about Ward's comment about squaring Mikko away. Maybe I would have to try it for, although she was as inquisitive as Taiho and could climb and jump as well as he, she never took the initiative. Like a respectful, ancient Chinese wife trotting after her husband, Mikko padded complacently behind her big brother. It drove me crazy. I made a silent vow: *I'll build up your self-confidence, little Mikko. Trust me.*

I repeated that promise a few minutes later at the kittens' dinner time.

"Din-din," I called, rattling the kitty-chow box. Instantly, as if they'd been born with the knowledge of what chow nuggets sound like, the kittens did an about-face and padded after me to the guest room, now re-named The Kitten Room. I put down the food and water, and, like proud parents, Ward and I stood back to watch the kittens chow down.

But we—especially myself—were in for a shock. For, after an inquisitive sniff at the food, Mikko backed off and sat down while Taiho strode to the bowl, growled his approval, and attacked the food with the gusto of a starving barbarian! Occasionally he glanced up to ensure that Mikko was in her place. She always was—passively sitting and watching her brother devour their lunch!

"Meeks!" I cried (unwittingly tagging her with one of many nicknames), "There's room for both of you. Haven't you ever heard of womens' lib?"

If she had, she wasn't saying, and though I tried to nudge her forward, her bottom was firmly planted.

When Taiho finally finished, he ambled away, but Mikko still sat.

"It's your turn, silly goose," I said.

But that stubborn little creature just watched and waited until Taiho stopped in the doorway and sat down to wash, a sign that he wasn't going back for seconds. Only then did Mikko approach the bowl to nibble delicately on his leftovers.

I was speechless with distress, but Ward howled. "Maybe one liberated female in the house is enough," he teased.

"Never! I'll teach that kitten to take her rightful place if it's the last thing I do," I declared.

Not long afterward, with their tummies round and full, the kittens finally showed signs of fatigue. Though they fought sleep—there was so much more to explore—their eyelids began to droop. Before giving in, with one last mighty effort, Taiho stumbled toward Ward on the sofa and half-climbed, half-jumped up to curl in a sleepy circle on Ward's lap.

My glance flew to Mikko. What would she do?

Crouched on the floor, she watched. She seemed so tiny and so alone. When I moved to pick her up, she edged away, not fearfully, just cautiously. "She's not ready to snuggle in yet," Ward said. "Ignore her. She'll come around."

I plunked down next to him and ruefully took in the scene—we three snuggled cozily together and Mikko hunched alone on the floor. I wondered, *Would she always be this way, slightly apart, always a step behind?*

As I pondered, Mikko slowly blinked, yawned, padded toward the sofa, and began to climb. She was weary and slow but didn't stop until she had toiled to the top of the back cushion. There she wriggled herself onto Ward's shoulder, nuzzled and licked his ear and, with a sigh, burrowed sleepily into the curve of his neck.

With a goofy smile, Ward tilted his head so that his cheek touched Mikko's fur. Her nestled, trusting position melted him.

I looked fondly at the three of them tucked together—my husband, the Bold One, and the Shy One. The Shy One? I chuckled. Maybe Mikko wasn't as self-assertive as I wished, but I had to hand it to her—she had a style of her own. She reminded me of Trushkie,

for, as young as she was, like Trushkie, she was an ul-
tra-feminine little kitten with the wiles of a Parisienne
coquette! I'd have to keep my eye on her. Maybe that
coy little creature could teach *me* a thing or two!

Fifteen

An Oscar Award-Winning Performance

"Ward, look! A 25-dollar refund from Mrs. Forrestert!" I brandished the letter and check that had just come in the mail. "It's a thank-you note for taking such good care of the kittens. Can you believe it?"

During the six months that we'd owned the kittens, at Mrs. Forrestert's request, we had kept her informed about their progress—their shots, neutering (which went smoothly, thank goodness) and their exuberant spirits. Her continued contact with us seemed unusual, but we didn't mind. In fact, like proud parents, we loved bragging about the kittens' antics, and Mrs. Forrestert loved hearing about them. She even admitted that she liked our names for them.

"I can visualize them perfectly!" she exclaimed when I described how the kittens would suddenly jump up to race frantically, back and forth, chasing invisible prey from the kitchen at the front of our house to the bedroom in the rear. On the carpeted portions, their racing paws pounded in muffled cadence, *thud-a-thud, thud-a-thud*. But when their flying bodies shot through the kitchen door and hurtled across the slippery floor, the thudding became a swoosh of flailing legs as the kittens caromed to a crash against the far wall. We'd cringe and gasp as those tiny, wild ones would just shake their heads like prize fighters who've gone down, but not for the full count, then, scrambling up, they'd careen off through the house again.

The note with the refund was the last we heard of Mrs. Forrestert. I'm sorry that I never got to tell her about Mikko's weird relationship with kitty-litter. She'd have laughed and loved it, for, to tell the truth, Mikko had a kitty-litter fetish. She went nuts—happily nuts—at the sound of litter being poured into the litter-box. The instant that her keen ears picked up the rustle of the litter bag being opened, she raced to the box. The first time that she did it, I had a momentary pang, remembering Donner and Tristan who had also been drawn to the sound of litter pouring as if it were the singing of sirens. But, whereas those two had sat like sentinels in the clouds of dust waiting to use the litter while it was still fresh, Mikko flung herself to the floor next to the box, rolling and twisting in drunken ecstasy as I poured the litter. Her face was pure joy and goofiness. The litter-sound affected her like pure catnip. Absolute bliss. Our dear little Mikko was a kitty-litter freak!

But listening to the litter and actually touching it were two, altogether different matters. Mikko refused to touch the litter unless it was absolutely necessary, and the contortions she went through to avoid it were bizarre. The poor little thing put off the call of nature as long as possible. When she couldn't wait a minute longer, she approached the box as if she were walking to the gallows. Then, standing outside of one corner of the box, with a fragile, curled paw and utmost delicacy, she scooped a shallow hole in the litter. As she did, her head was turned aside, nose wrinkled and mouth turned down with distaste. She then turned, aimed her tiny rear at the corner of the box, backed up to it in a scooting motion, and, with extreme care, raised up all four of her paws, one at a time, rear ones first, to grasp the edges of the box. And there she perched, clinging tenaciously, swaying slightly, her bony little rear end hanging out over the litter and her upper body thrust forward for balance—like a circus bear teetering on a beach ball. Her brow was so furrowed in concentration that her eyes narrowed to dark slits. When her business was finished, she hopped down, turned, and as fastidiously and quickly as possible, tossed a dainty dusting of litter over her mess. After shaking her paw to rid it of the tiniest grain of litter, she slipped away. Her delicate instincts must have been terribly bruised by Taiho's flamboyant and robust approach to the litter-box. You could practically hear him cry *Gung-ho!* as he plunged in, flung litter hither and yon, and vigorously dug a gigantic hole. When finished, he swung his paw through the litter with broad, sweeping strokes to cover his mess, then bounded off, scattering clouds of dust in his wake.

Taiho wasn't just a macho little guy. He was also a natural-born actor. If Academy Awards were given to cats, Taiho would have an Oscar on his mantelpiece, for he was, without question, the Laurence Olivier of felines. I discovered his talent in the "Affair of the In-jured Eye."

The injury occurred late one Sunday night when the kittens were about eight months old, during one of their vigorous wrestling matches. In the scuffle, Taiho was wounded—mortally wounded, you would have thought, to hear him squawk about it. The fact was, Mikko had accidentally scratched his eye.

We rushed to help him, but, shrieking, he dashed under the sofa and huddled there, crying piteously for one or two minutes before becoming ominously silent. Lying on our stomachs, we peered at him. He was hunched as low and as far away from us as he could get. One eye glared fiercely. The other was squeezed closed.

When he refused to budge, even for bribes of tuna fish, we shoved the sofa aside. To our surprise, without a murmur, Taiho let me pick him up. When he turned his face toward us, we were shocked. His eye was pink, puffy, and steadily swelling.

I spent the night on the bathroom floor, cradling Taiho and bathing his eye with warm, wet compresses and crooning softly to him. But, by morning, the eye was worse; the third eyelid, gray and slick, had slid over the eyeball. Although I knew that the lid was automatically acting to cover and protect Taiho's eye, its looks were scary and made the eye look even worse. I was sick with worry that Taiho would go blind.

The vet's receptionist must have heard the panic in my voice over the phone and agreed to squeeze Taiho into the doctor's schedule. If I'd been face-to-face with her, in gratitude, I'd have covered her hands with kisses.

The trip to the clinic was painful. Taiho huddled in the corner of his carrier, uttering occasional pitiful mews. I could hardly see through my tears. "Tai, Tai," I murmured over and over, hoping that my low tones would comfort him.

A few minutes later, the doctor's words comforted me. "Don't worry. It looks a lot worse than it is," he assured me with a smile. "It's fairly common for cats to scratch their eyes when they tussle. With some ointment he'll be fine in a few days."

I was so relieved that in the car I let my forehead drop down on the steering wheel and burst into sobs.

Applying ointment to Taiho's eye was a lot easier than giving him pills. Our sad, puffy-eyed invalid accepted my ministrations without a fuss. As a reward for his good behavior, I pampered Taiho with tidbits of his favorite foods—chicken paprika, Boursin cheese, and butterscotch-ripple ice cream. Mikko, of course, demanded her share of treats and attention by shrill squawking as only Siamese can. She kept her distance from Taiho and refused to snuggle with him as long as a whiff of ointment lingered.

During the first day, Taiho accepted my offerings in stoic silence. Gradually, however, as the swelling went down, he roused himself to murmur his thanks, and, with his good eye, to cast a baleful look of gratitude my way. I didn't know it at the time, but the actor in Taiho was stirring.

By the third day, the patient was well enough to roll over and luxuriate in my sympathetic crooning and chin-and-tummy scratching. Life, for Taiho, had become much more than just snacks of chicken, cheese, and ice cream; life had become a bowl of cherries—and Taiho was gorging himself on the fruit.

As the vet had assured me, Taiho's eye healed perfectly. It was time to return to a normal life. Out with the snacks, in with vitamin-fortified cat food. Both kittens grumbled at the change and tried to coax treats from me by joining forces in countless figure eights around my ankles, but I was made of sterner stuff than I had been three years earlier when I had let Trushkie dictate the menu, and her tummy had paid the price for my weakness. Now, I faced the kittens with my arms folded across my chest. "No more snacks. It's back to nutritious foods for the two of you," I declared. They cocked their heads and appraised me with solemn eyes. *Did I really mean it?* Yes… my body language spoke volumes. After a few seconds, they accepted the inevitable and, with resigned sighs, dutifully settled in to chow down on cat food.

As far as Ward and I were concerned, the incident of the injury was over. We forgot the whole episode.

But Taiho did not.

One morning a month later, looking for a bit of action, Taiho jogged into the bedroom where Mikko and I were performing our morning bed-making ritual: I would flap and wave the bedsheets high in the air and, with squeaky yelps of joy, Mikko would dive in and out of their undulating folds. Usually, Taiho disdained this frivolous activity; he preferred more physical combat with large cardboard boxes that needed to be pummeled and upended and explored. But Mikko's flying body—and the fact that she didn't know she was being stalked—made her irresistible.

Taiho sprang. He plunged into the billowing sheets. Whack! His head collided with my hand—and my finger poked his eye!

Everything happened in a microsecond. Taiho crash-dived to the floor and, howling, he raced from the room, looking for cover.

I hurtled after him, horrified, frantic, apologizing over and over. "Oh, Taiho! I'm so sorry! Let me see your eye! Oh, Tai! Tai!"

Taiho took refuge under the coffee table. Momentarily it struck me that he was "hiding" in a very accessible spot. *If he had wanted to be left alone, why hadn't he raced for the farthest corner under the bed?* But the thought was fleeting and flashed out of my mind as I crawled after him.

Just as before, when his eye was injured, Taiho huddled pathetically in ominous silence. One eye was squeezed shut. The right eye! The same one!

His left eye, unblinking, stared reprovingly at me.

I was heartsick as I watched this lovely, wounded cat. At that moment his squinty eye opened just a slit—to let a tear roll down his nose. Oh, my God! My heart wrenched. The pain of it! Slowly I reached out to draw Taiho to me. To my surprise, he didn't back away but, instead, hunched toward me with soft, piteous cries. Another wondering thought flashed through my mind: *Don't injured animals usually want to be left alone?*

Gently I stroked Taiho's neck, hoping to relax him so that I could look at his injury.

Then I stopped. Just a minute. Something was unusual. Then I realized—Taiho was purring! It was a muted tremolo, deep-down inside. It was so faint that I didn't actually hear it but felt its vibrations with my fingertips. I knew that animals sometimes purr even in pain, even when dying—but, as I held this little vibrating creature, I sensed that these were purrs of pure contentment. Then I realized that Taiho, the actor, was "on stage." Oh, I didn't doubt that his eye smarted a bit from the poke, but certainly not enough to warrant his crumpled pose and devastatingly wounded look.

I chuckled. "Okay, I'll go along with your act." And, as I cradled him in my arms, I continued my crooning and petting. Within seconds of nestling in, Taiho pushed his purr to full throttle. It boomed out with pure joy—and blew his whole act.

Apparently Taiho didn't realize this because he continued his dramatics, lying limply and gazing up at me with his "good" eye. How he gloried in my fervent apologies and whispered sweet talk. The more I murmured, the louder he purred, and the more limp he became.

Then, just when I thought he had sunk into an ecstatic trance, he opened his "bad" eye. For a long moment it looked straight at me—clear, bright, and healthy. Then, both eyes closed in ecstasy.

The game was up, and now both of us knew it. Yet we remained silently there, Taiho and I. A gentle smile softened Taiho's face. Maybe, because he liked having his tummy rubbed. Maybe, in anticipation of butterscotch-ripple ice cream.

Or maybe, it was the self-satisfied smile of an actor who knows that he has just given an Oscar-winning performance.

Sixteen

"We Are Siamese…
If You Please"

It was late on a Sunday afternoon. The house was unusually quiet. I stood in the living room doorway and sighed. Talk about a lived-in look! Our friends' homes were tastefully decorated in Early American, Modern, or Traditional. Ours was more like "Contemporary Cat."

Doorknobs were draped with dangling cords for Taiho and Mikko to bat, prancing and feinting like boxers at their punching bags. Cat toys lay scattered about like debris washed ashore after a storm. Balls of every size and color peeked from under chairs, from behind draperies, and clustered in corners—ping-pong balls, rubber balls, balls of crushed wax paper or aluminum foil, and rainbow-colored plastic balls with rattley little bells inside. A large, crinkled, brown paper bag lay like a collapsed balloon in the middle of the rug. It was the cats' all-purpose bag, for napping in, for jumping out of to ambush passing ankles, and for suddenly pouncing upon, just in case an enemy lurked inside. Two, sturdy, molting scratching posts, like shaggy sentinels, flanked the sofa. Further littering the scene, and adding a touch of poignancy, were the strewn corpses of limp, red, blue, and yellow catnip mice.

We had both sets of parents to thank for this abundance of mice. When they *finally* accepted the fact that we were going to enrich their lives with grandkittens instead of grandchildren, they flung themselves wholeheartedly into the "grandparent thing." They bombarded us with kitty toys, kitty snacks, and enough catnip mice to keep Taiho and Mikko on an herbal high for weeks. Prancing on their haunches in a cloud of "*eau de catnip,*" the cats buffeted the stuffed little critters unmercifully around the room in spirited games of mouse-soccer. Or, as mighty hunters, they stalked and cornered the mice. Then, with growls of victory, they hunched above their prey, gnawing and slobbering them until their little mouse seams split and their frayed tails were shredded to ratty strings.

Now, as I viewed the room, I had to admit that, despite the clutter, it was a scene of contentment. Mikko and Taiho, snuggled cozily together, were snoozing in a patch of late afternoon sunshine. Sprawled, half asleep, on the nearby sofa, with an open book on his chest, Ward was lazily watching the cats from under drooping eyelids.

Just then, Mikko stirred, uncoiled, and languidly stretched, her slender back forming a graceful arc and the muscles of her rear legs so elongated that they quivered delicately. Her stretch was as contagious as a yawn, and Taiho now stretched out his front legs and began to knead his paws against Mikko's tummy. Ward shifted position, rotated his neck and shoulders, and uttered satisfied groans.

"What a lazy bunch!" I declared.

Ward grunted. "You're just jealous. Come on, join us." He patted the sofa. As I burrowed in, both cats cast me a groggy, welcoming look.

I laughed. "They're lovely, aren't they?" I said.

"Mmmmmm," Ward murmured, half asleep.

"They've grown up into real beauties. Remember how roly-poly they were?" I asked.

"Mmmmm." Ward's response was barely audible.

No matter. I studied the groggy gang. As the sunlight crept across the carpet, Mikko and Taiho shifted and moved sleepily with it. Once again I marveled at how the cats had matured, gradually changing from frolicking kittens to gangly-legged juveniles, and then to mature, stylish Siamese beauties.

Taiho was larger and more solid than Mikko, but both cats were firm-muscled, and both were graceful, with long necks, perky, wide-set ears, and deep-blue eyes. Those eyes, which had once been wide with innocence and wonder, now gleamed with oriental intelligence and mystery.

Burnished by the sunlight, the cats' fine-textured fur seemed sculpted to their sleek bodies, and their dark, glossy masks, ears, legs, and tails contrasted hand-

somely with the shades of fawn and ivory on their
backs, chests, and tummies.

Despite their maturity, the cats hadn't lost their
lively curiosity. We loved it when, without warning,
they'd leap up, a-quiver with excitement, and race off
to explore every nook and cranny of the apartment as
if they'd just been plunked down on alien soil. With
what zeal they investigated! Their noses twitched, ears
perked, mouths hung half-open to fully relish every
scent, and their tails waved joyously like wind-whipped
flags! I grinned, remembering how, at times, bursting
with such passion for life, they'd stop short, and turn
to us, heads cocked and eyes shining. *Ain't life grand?*
they seemed to exclaim.

Leaning over, I ran my fingertips across Mikko's
tummy and smiled at her tiny moan of pleasure. "You
love that, don't you, Mikko?" I murmured.

That bit of attention was all she needed. Purring
at full volume, she squirmed and pushed her head
against my hand, an invitation—a demand—for a forehead massage. "Okay, okay," I laughed and firmly
circled my fingertips above her blissfully closed eyes.

I considered the shape of the cats' heads. No longer
round and kittenish, they were now triangular with
classic profiles that ran in an unbroken line from forehead to chin. "You know, kitties," I whispered, "you
are *très, très chic.*" They replied with a purr. *But of
course... we're Siamese.*

I nudged Ward. "Doesn't it bother you that Mikko
is so dependent on us—especially on me?"

The question roused Ward. "Too dependent? What're you talking about? She's just an unusually loving cat," he said. "She's great. In fact, she's perfect," he added with emphasis.

"Well, sometimes I feel like I'm a shrine at which Mikko worships," I replied. "I guess I should be flattered, but it's weird."

"You're weird," Ward answered with a grin. "And you're imagining things."

No, I wasn't. I knew it. Mikko was literally my shadow. Ruth to my Naomi. "Whither thou goest, I shall go…." She walked so closely behind me that if I stopped short, she rammed her nose into my calf. When I ironed, she huddled at my feet and purred. She insisted on being face-to-face as much as possible. When I sat down to read, she'd spring to my armrest with a squeaky little cry. There she'd perch, her ears forward and alert, her body upright, leaning slightly toward me, one leg raised with its paw delicately drooping in a balletic pose. With her nose ten inches from mine, she embraced me with her eyes. *I love you madly*, her expression said. Mikko was a soft cat. Everything about her was soft—her eyes, her body, her expression, and her personality.

Mikko's adoration continued at night. When I got into bed, Mikko sprang lightly to my chest, where she snuggled and purred. It was impossible to deny her. The love that radiated from her took me prisoner and melted my heart. Ward was probably right. Mikko *was* perfect.

Well, no—not quite perfect, I reminded myself, for I was still distressed by Mikko's unassertive nature. I admire independence. It bothered me that Mikko didn't have an independent spirit. What's more, she didn't seem to care. I tried so hard to teach her to assert herself, especially in her relationship with Taiho, but she never lost her unseemly (to me) deference to him. That charming little female cat simply was not interested in Women's Lib or equal rights. How ironic that Mikko was *my* cat, I who practically bowed every time I passed the copy of the Equal Rights Amendment which I'd posted on the refrigerator.

One day, totally exasperated, I held Mikko up to let her take a good look at the Amendment, but she pretended not to see it. However, she had a grand time batting magnets off of the fridge door.

"You're hopeless, Mikko," I sighed and set her down.

Mikko sighed, too, with love—and nuzzled my ankle.

Taiho's independent spirit more than made up for Mikko's lack of it. He had enough for a half-dozen cats. Like Mikko, Taiho would sit and gaze adoringly at us—*if he felt like it*. He'd even come when called—*if he felt like it*. Taiho could do anything *as long as he felt like it!* But mostly, he swaggered around a lot or "honored" Ward by sauntering to him and leaping to his lap with a regal air that proclaimed, *Lucky man, I've chosen you to sit with.*

Taiho's lordliness toward Ward was merely for theatrical effect, a reminder of his acting skills. In fact,

Ward was Taiho's hero. The two were inseparable, not in the nose-rubbing girlish way that Mikko and I were but in typical male fashion. They expressed their feelings with lots of swatting, batting, and rough-housing that ended when Taiho assumed his "chin low, rump high" posture—neck extended, chin flattened on the floor and rear end pointed heavenward, the signal for Ward to scratch the end of his spine. The moment that Ward did, Taiho collapsed, melting into a goofily happy cat whose throaty purr could put a torch singer to shame.

The togetherness that Taiho and I shared during his eye injuries—both the genuine and the phoney ones—was special, but it was Ward with whom this macho cat bonded like Crazy Glue.

Three years passed quickly. Mikko and Taiho seemed to prove the theory that cats who've had secure, happy kittenhoods mature into mentally and emotionally healthy adults. We were eventually to discover that there can be exceptions to this rule, but at the time we knew that if we gave Mikko and Taiho one of those "How Healthy Is Your Ego?" quizzes—the kind you find in pop psychology magazines—they'd pass *summa cum laude*.

One indication of the cats' mental health was their running, Siamese chatter. They commented on everything with growls, squeaks, mumbles, and yowls of delight. Ambling into the kitchen to find a hearty breakfast, they chirruped their approval. However, if breakfast wasn't ready, they'd grumble, scold me, and let me know that my negligence was intolerable.

Both cats rushed to report lots of things to us—a dandy squirrel in the yard, a marvelous sock they'd found under the bed, an accidental tidbit of cheese on the kitchen floor. They told us everything. And when they had nothing specific to report, prattling, they padded after us, remarking loudly on the state of affairs in general. Our friends asked how we could stand such constant "squawking and caterwauling." We loved it. It was unique Siamese chatter. And, to the cats' delight, we chattered right back.

Mikko's babble was as soft and sweet as poetry. Partnered with soulful gazes, her tiny mews were like love sonnets. When she pleaded plaintively for treats, she dramatized her pathos with a raised, tucked paw. Her act was worthy of a wandering, Tibetan monk. She lacked only a begging bowl.

Taiho was too macho for love sonnets. Taiho was a strongly opinionated orator who expressed his views whether asked for them or not. He trumpeted his likes in roars of joy, his dislikes in screeches of indignation, and his demands in deep-throated, head-thrown-back howls for attention. Entering a room, Taiho would first pause dramatically in the doorway, announcing his arrival with a bellow before strutting in to monopolize the conversation. Modesty was not his strong suit.

When describing Mikko to others, naturally, we spoke of her delicacy, dependency, her need to be gently cared for, and the irresistible "lost soul" look in her eyes. When describing Taiho, our tones firmed as we bragged about his bravado, his all-American spirit of independence, his strutting stride, and proud posture.

So, it was a surprise when, six months after that peaceful living room scene, an incident occurred that completely flipped many of our notions about the cats.

Seventeen

It Takes Two To Travel

"It's finally happened," Ward announced as he swung through the doorway, waving a sheaf of papers. He was excited, but even so, I heard a hint of regret in his voice, and I knew that his orders had arrived—orders to the Pentagon. It's almost impossible to have a naval career without serving, at least once, in that vast, fortress-like building in Virginia.

"It's a great job assignment," he continued. "But, you know...." His voice trailed off, and we both thought of what this assignment meant—selling our house in Columbia, Maryland, and moving closer to the Pentagon, 25 miles away. Some people made that miserable, daily commute as a trade-off to living in Columbia's village atmosphere with its woodlands and lakes. Ward tried the commute for a while, but the rush-hour traffic was exhausting and frustrating. We began to look for a place in Virginia, and, in a stroke of good luck, we soon found a charming, three-story townhouse only four miles from the Pentagon.

The Navy's "Household To-Do" list, designed to help make our move relatively stress-free, reminded us to send out change-of-address cards, to cancel utilities, newspaper delivery, and so forth. As far as I was concerned, that was easy, stress-free stuff. What did stress me was the item that I added to the list: How to transport the cats to the new house.

On the kittens' first-ride from Mrs. Forrestert's home to ours, Mikko and Taiho had been too bewildered—and too tiny—to put up much of a fuss, but as they had grown, they'd become belligerently anti-car cats. Our trips to the vet, only a mile away, were high adventures, action-packed and tension-filled. The instant that the cats saw me take their cage from the closet, they scattered like hurricane-blown leaves. When we finally trapped them and pushed them inside, they screeched, glowered, rattled the bars, and banged their heads repeatedly against the door. The only way that I could manage the drive without going mad was to put the cage out of sight on the back seat and grit my teeth until my jaws ached. And that was for one mile. Could I cope—and could the cats survive—a 25-mile drive? I put the question to our vet.

"No problem. We'll tranquilize them," he replied. My shoulders slumped in relief. With two, tranquil cats flaked out in the back seat, I figured we could do this move with one hand tied behind our backs.

When you're as cocky as I was, you deserve punishment. And I got it—in spades.

The day of the move began with a traumatic battle to give the cats their tranquilizer pills. I didn't know it then, but it was a harbinger of things to come. I was no more expert at pill "administration" than I had been in Germany. Like Donner and Tristan, when faced with pills, Mikko and Taiho clamped their jaws shut and glared at me. When I did manage to ram a pill between their clenched teeth, they knew the trick of hiding it in their cheeks, then spitting it out with a triumphant sneer. (Are all cats born with this knowledge?) This time, however, with a frightening 25-mile drive at stake, I was far more determined than they, and, finally, I stroked the pills down their protesting throats.

We drove in a two-car caravan, both cars packed with household "basics" to tide us over the first few days in the townhouse. The cats and I were in the first car. Ward followed, as rear guard. My back seat was crammed with boxes from floor to ceiling, so the cats' cage had to go on the front passenger seat. I was nervous about it, but I put my faith in the tranquilizers, which, according to the vet, would keep the cats drowsy and woozy for three or four hours. I relaxed when I peered into the cage and saw that, although both cats were struggling to sit, they were sinking on wobbly legs. As they drooped, they mumbled very nasty things at us under their breath. (I had no idea they knew that kind of language!)

The cats continued to mumble as I headed south on Route 29. After three or four miles, glancing into the cat carrier, I was surprised to see that they were still moving—restlessly tossing and turning. I'd expected them to be zonked by now.

Then it happened. There was a heaven-shattering screech, and a claw squeezed out through the wire mesh. I was so shocked that I jumped and momentarily lost control of the steering wheel. The car lurched. I recovered quickly, but my heart pounded in my throat when I saw that both cats were upright, their bodies rigid. They were howling and trying to escape with heavy, drunken lunges at the bars of the cage.

"Mikko, Taiho, it's all right… it's all right," I reassured them over and over. But I might as well have been crying into a whirling wind, for instead of being calmed by my voice, the cats became wild creatures with rolling, frantic eyes. They screeched and clawed at the cage. They spit at me, flinging strings of saliva from their mouths. Taiho shoved his paw out farther through the narrow bars and slashed my arm. It stung. I cried out. Blood trickled onto my jeans.

I was terrified. Traffic was heavy. I couldn't pull over safely. Besides, my senses were in such a whirl that I couldn't think clearly. I was aware only of the rampaging cats. To keep out of range of those fierce, waving claws, I cowered as far away as possible. Behind me, Ward was alarmed by my erratic driving but could do nothing except to follow closely.

The cats raged for all 25 miles, though, thankfully, by the time I pulled up in front of the townhouse, their screeches had dwindled with fatigue to hoarse growls. Their forelegs, poking through the wires, were limp except for sporadic jerks and straining of their claws.

Screeching to a halt behind me, Ward jumped from his car and raced over to find me slumped across the steering wheel, trembling and drenched with sweat. I gasped out the story. Then, holding the cage between us at arm's length, we carried it into the front hallway.

I was sure that the cats were too exhausted to move, but the instant that we opened the cage door, they shot out like twin bullets. For a moment, they crouched and froze in the new surroundings. Their eyes searched wildly for cover, but there wasn't a stick of furniture. Then, they raced frantically from room to room, like hunted animals, bellies low to the ground. They flew so fast that they lost control, skidding across the bare, wooden floors. The sound of their scrabbling claws echoed through the barren rooms.

We followed, futilely calling their names. But they were too quick, too frightened. At the top of the steps to the unlit basement, they paused for a fraction of a second, then slithered down, quickly but warily, their tensed bodies pressed close to the wall, their ears perked. Instinctively, they raced to the farthest, darkest corner and huddled there. Their wild eyes, peering through the gloom, warned us not to come a step closer.

Ward and I slumped on the bottom step and stared in alarm at the two terrified cats. What had happened? What had gone wrong? Had they somehow managed to spit out the tranquilizers? All our careful planning had gone haywire. We later learned that sometimes tranquilizers can cause animals to go berserk, but at that moment, we understood nothing. It was a nightmare. I wondered if we'd ever regain Mikko's and Taiho's love and trust. Suddenly, all of the tenseness of the last two hours drained from me like water being sucked into a whirlpool. I sagged against Ward and sobbed uncontrollably.

For a half-hour we cooed softly to the cats, trying to coax them to us. As still as statues, they hunched together and stared blankly at us. Not a muscle twitched. Finally, deciding that we had stressed them enough for one day, we set out food, water, and kitty-litter and left them alone, to emerge when they were ready. We hoped that the sounds of our moving about upstairs would rouse their curiosity.

It was 24 hours before a cautious, inquisitive nose peeked above the basement stairway. "Tai… " I started to exclaim, then stopped. It wasn't Taiho the Bold. It was Mikko the Meek! I was amazed that she had taken the initiative to come up first. I was even more amazed to see that Taiho was still downstairs, huddled in the corner.

For ten minutes, Mikko edged her way slowly into the room, her neck straining forward, every sense alert. I fought an impulse to sweep her into my arms and smother her with kisses. After another hour of cautious exploring, she allowed me to approach and stroke her, but, even then, her muscles were tense, ready for flight. By nightfall, she trusted us enough to join us on our air mattress, but she curled up alone at the bottom at the very edge.

For the next 24 hours, Taiho the Bold crouched miserably in his corner. I could hardly eat or sleep. I checked on him constantly. Ward, equally concerned, phoned from work two or three times.

By the morning of the third day I couldn't stand it another minute. Taiho needed to be brought back into the family fold. With determined steps, I went downstairs and settled in on the floor near him. For almost an hour, while Taiho fixed me with a baleful stare, I crooned and whispered to him while edging closer and closer until I could reach out and brush my fingertip against his cheek. I thought that he might growl or slink away. Instead, at my touch, Taiho's taut muscles instantly slackened. The fear in his eyes softened to gratefulness. My own eyes misted as, slowly, whimpering low, Taiho inched his crouching body toward my lap.

"Tai, Tai," I cried and leaned over to bury my face in his fur.

It took another half-hour of soothing words and gentle stroking before Taiho was ready to go upstairs. I led the way, followed, circumspectly, by this elegant cat who had fooled us with his swagger but who was a vulnerable, frightened little fellow at heart.

Considering their traumatic introduction to the new house, Mikko and Taiho adapted with surprising speed. They found that racing up and down three flights of steps in a townhouse was as much fun—and more challenging—as dashing back and forth on a straight path in a one-story house. They loved our postage-stamp, fenced-in yard where they lazed in the sun, nibbled on tender grass, and futilely chased the occasional chipmunks who whizzed through.

One day, during Taiho's and Mikko's annual physical exam, the vet surprised me with a tiny toothbrush and a sample tube of fish-flavored toothpaste. "Start brushing the cats' teeth once a week," he said. "If you don't, there's a greater chance of their having inflamed gums and losing their teeth when they're older—and, of course, pain."

We had read about toothbrushing in The Book, but had dismissed it—with a twinge of guilt—as too bothersome. Now, remembering the horrid, spit-flying saga of Donner's and Tristan's blue deworming pills, I felt my pulse sprint alarmingly at the prospect of fooling around again in cats' mouths.

"It's not difficult, and some cats actually like it," the doctor added and gave me instructions for a three-step course: Toothbrushing of Cats 101.

That night Ward watched, amused, while I launched Dental Hygiene for Cats. I began with Taiho, who purred merrily when I pulled him up to my lap, and purred louder still when I put a dab of toothpaste on his lip—"step one." To me, the paste had the faint odor of rotten herring, but, to Taiho, it was the aroma of a holiday dinner. His eyes sparkled as he craned his head, searching for the source of that gourmet paste. When I dabbed a bit more onto his eager lips, his elastic tongue swiveled out to lick his chops so heartily you'd have thought he'd eaten a whole tuna. He gazed up at me with love. *You wonderful woman*, he growled contentedly.

Taking advantage of his relaxed smile, cautiously I went on to "step two." The vet's calm, sane words of advice echoed in my brain. "Lightly touch the cat's teeth and gums with the tip of a cotton swab that's been dipped in toothpaste."

I might as well have tried to ram a rolling pin in Taiho's mouth. At the first touch of the swab, he stiffened, sputtered, and wriggled from my lap with the speed and agility of an eel. Then he stood in the doorway, his fur ruffled in indignation. He shot me a killer look. *Scheming woman*, it said. *Oh, you are not to be trusted!* With that he turned and stalked from the room, striding past a startled Mikko.

"Wow!" Ward laughed as we watched Taiho make his irate exit. "Obviously Taiho is not one of those rare cats who like toothbrushing."

I sighed, reached for Mikko and, with apprehension, began with "step one."

I was prepared for a repeat performance, but from the moment of "step one," then "step two," and, finally, "step three," which consisted of swishing the small, super-soft toothbrush in Mikko's mouth, it was crystal-clear—Mikko was a toothbrushing addict! Propped in my lap with her mouth relaxed and slack, she reveled in the delicate tingle of the brush on her teeth and in the gentle massage of the cotton swab— and sometimes my little finger—on her gums. With her eyes closed in rapture, she gushed purrs of thanks.

Not wanting the peaceful moment to end, when I finished with her teeth, I slid my fingers up to Mikko's forehead and stroked in small circles above her eyes.

As I did, I felt her body slump against mine. I moved my fingers, still circling, up and behind her ears. More slumping. Slowly, with the probing fingers of a masseuse, I worked my way down Mikko's spine, ending with a leisurely tug along the length of her tail. That did it. Like a pampered matron at a spa, Mikko sighed and splayed her limp, happy body across my lap. I swear I heard her whisper, *More.*

Mikko's "spa treatments" became so much of a ritual that I should have painted our front door bright red à la Elizabeth Arden salons. Mikko wasn't the only one who benefited from our relaxation therapy. I, too, fell under the calm, healing spell of loving interaction with a trusting and contented cat. I didn't check my blood pressure after our massage sessions, but I suspect it idled down to a slow, mellow beat.

As for Taiho, he eventually let me brush his teeth; he recognized a determined woman when he met one. I suspect he even came to enjoy the gentle gum massage and the overall body rub, for I gave him the same "spa treatment." To preserve his macho image, however, Taiho couldn't afford to admit that he'd been wrong at first, and I imagine that, behind my back, he grumbled about me in a tough guy tone to impress Mikko.

Three years passed so quickly that I was surprised when Ward reminded me that it was almost time to move on to his next assignment. When his orders arrived a month later, we were thrilled to see our destination—Hawaii!

Sun-drenched, flower-bedecked Hawaii! A tropical paradise. Time was short. We had only seven weeks to prepare to leave. We popped a champagne cork and danced around the kitchen. From the doorway, Mikko and Taiho watched our craziness with cocked heads and expectant looks because sometimes when Ward and I celebrated, we tossed bits of Swiss cheese or shrimp their way.

"Hawaii, kitties!" I called. "You'll love it. Lots of sunshine to loll about in." But the cats weren't interested. This celebration obviously didn't involve Swiss cheese or shrimp, so they shrugged and strolled over to the window where a puddle of sunshine awaited them.

With growing excitement, we pored over the Hawaiian brochures that had come with Ward's orders when, suddenly, our visions of white-sand beaches and hula dances were shattered by two short sentences. They struck us an unexpected blow. *"Hawaii is free of rabies. To maintain this condition, all pets entering the state must remain in quarantine for four months."*

Stunned, we gaped at one another. Mikko and Taiho! Our heads swiveled in unison toward the cats. Four months! In a cage! It was bad enough that they'd have to endure the long flight to Hawaii in the hold of a plane. Then, four months in quarantine! It was a sobering revelation.

For a month, as we prepared our household goods, we brooded. Our excitement was overshadowed by worry. What if we left the cats here? If we did, could we find a home for them? Not just any home, but a great home. Could we bear to part with them? Then, again, if we did take them, and if they did tolerate the flight without ill effects, how would they react to the quarantine? Day and night the questions ran through our minds. Still we procrastinated, and my head throbbed almost constantly.

Ward finally forced the issue. One night, after dinner, he pulled me down beside him on the sofa. "We have to face it. We're getting down to the wire," he said solemnly. "Do we take them or not?"

I looked numbly at him. I couldn't answer. But he was right. We had to make a decision—*now*.

Eighteen

If This Is Hawaii, Where Are The Hula Dancers?

The clerk at the airline check-in counter pressed a button, and the baggage conveyor belt hummed to life. I caught my breath. Instinctively my hand flew up to stop the belt. I didn't, of course. Instead, with pounding temples, I watched as our large, gunmetal-gray cat carrier, holding a terrified pair of cats, rumbled along the belt toward the baggage area, the opening of which, with its black, rubbery flaps looked like a voracious maw.

As the carrier passed us on its way to the hold of the Hawaii-bound plane, we had our last glimpse of Mikko and Taiho through the wire mesh door. Jouncing into the unknown, rigid with fear, they cowered together, their eyes wild and wide. In that last moment before the carrier entered the baggage room, the cats also glimpsed us. They shrieked—shrill, desperate, ear-splitting Siamese squawks that knifed through the airport's conversational drone and chilled us to the marrow. Their eyes begged us to release them. Then, just as the flaps engulfed the carrier, as if greedily suck-ing it in, Taiho made a desperate cage-rattling lunge against the wire door. I gave a cry and lurched toward him. But then the carrier was gone. My cry sank to a low moan as I stared at the empty, relentlessly rolling conveyor belt. With a chill, I recalled all the horror stories we'd heard of pets suffering in dark, cold, air-craft holds.

Turning me around and taking my arm, Ward led me toward the exit. We weren't going to Hawaii on the cats' plane. They were going on ahead of us because for the next six weeks Ward and I would be living in a motel in Florida while Ward attended a special Navy school. It would be six weeks before we could join the cats in the Islands!

Our decision to send the cats to Hawaii had come after a long conversation that night when Ward had sat me down on the sofa and forced me to face the necessity of making up our minds. Reluctantly we de-cided to run a newspaper ad offering the cats to a good home—a "great home," I insisted. Failing that, we would take them with us and pray that they'd survive the flight and the long quarantine, particularly the first six weeks when they'd be there alone.

Five people answered our ad. All of them claimed to adore cats and all raved about Mikko's and Taiho's beauty, but not one sank spontaneously to his knees to stroke and cuddle the cats.

"How can any true cat-lover just stand there and not make any attempt to pet the cats?" I asked incredulously. "It doesn't make sense."

We decided that if we couldn't find a person who was as passionate and enamored by Mikko and Taiho as we were, someone who wanted to swoop them up and take them home that very minute, we would not give them up.

While we waited nervously for further responses to the ad, a letter from Hawaii changed everything. It came from the most wonderful people: Navy Commander Dave Gill and his wife, Julie, the couple who had been assigned as our sponsors (support groups for newcomers) in Hawaii. The Gills had already sent us a big packet of information about Ward's new duty station. Now, in a letter that brought tears to my eyes, they offered to help with Mikko and Taiho. They loved cats, they wrote. They promised to meet Mikko's and Taiho's plane and to visit them regularly in quarantine until our arrival. Further, they assured us that the quarantine station was a well-run, clean place with cages large enough for people to go inside and play with their pets. The Gills' letter made it much easier to reach a decision. Another, very easy decision was: *No tranquilizers!*

The cats survived the flight, and, true to their word, Dave and Julie visited Mikko and Taiho regularly, bearing toys and kitty treats as if they were offerings to royalty. Their description of the cats' cage cheered us.

It was a large walk-in cage, half-enclosed, and half-open to the tropical breezes. They reported that after a couple of very timid days, Mikko had warmed up to them, but Taiho was still wary and eyed them suspiciously from a corner of the cage. "He needs a little more time to adjust, but he'll be fine," Julie wrote.

We nodded over the Gills' letter. It made sense in the light of Taiho's reaction to moving to the townhouse. Still, when I remembered how he'd cowered in a corner of the basement, I imagined him hunched in a corner of the quarantine cage. The image broke my heart. "They need us. They really need us," I sighed and impatiently counted the days until our departure.

Our arrival in Hawaii was so rushed that I can barely remember deplaning and collecting our luggage. Julie was at work and couldn't meet us. Dave, crying "Aloha!" tossed gorgeous flower *leis* around our necks, then announced that he had to take Ward directly to his new duty station. We had arrived in the middle of a crisis, fondly known as a "flap." (How often I was to hear that word!) Ward was to jump right in! There was just time to drop me off at our house before they dashed off to their flap.

The bungalow that would be our home for the next three years, a plain, long, low, wooden building with a tin roof, was ringed with bright tropical flowers and lush ferns. Feathery hibiscus blazed at the back door. Several brilliant birds of paradise graced the side yard, and shiny, sword-like leaves of variegated colors grew in thick clumps beneath the windows. Two sweet-scented plumeria trees on the front lawn were so heavy with white blossoms that they resembled clouds. In the gentle breeze, occasional blossoms dropped lightly to the grass. The backyard was completely shadowed by a massive monkeypod tree whose wide-sweeping branches, dripping with long, thin nut-brown pods, overarched the screened-in patio at the rear. Dotting the yard were six, slim, 40-foot high coconut palms, their green nuts thickly clustered beneath the swaying umbrella of softly rustling palm leaves. Inside, I discovered that the Gills had made the beds, stocked the kitchen with some staples, and adorned the coffee table with welcoming flowers and champagne. I was eager to explore our bit of Hawaiian paradise, but was even more eager to see the cats. I took a long, delicious sniff of the bouquet, popped the champagne into the fridge, grabbed a map of the island, and then I also dashed—to the bus stop! To the cats!

I had lived in Hawaii when I, myself, was in the Navy before I was married, but I knew nothing of the quarantine station. My map showed that it was way out in the boondocks. Sure enough, after rattling along for half an hour, the bus finally ground to a halt. "Your stop," the driver said.

My stop? We were surrounded by uninhabited, dry, scrubby ground. The driver pointed toward a low mountain. "Short walk, straight ahead," he said.

Short walk! For fifteen minutes I plodded uphill on an unpaved road. It was the dry season. Every footstep kicked up puffs of brick-red dust. A passing pick-up truck shrouded me in blinding clouds of it.

The station, however, was an oasis, a compound of low, long buildings shaded by palms and monkeypod trees with masses of red hibiscus flowers brightening the entrance. My pulse raced as I followed Nancy, a young staffer, to the cat section.

The station resembled a small zoo. The rows of cages lining narrow pathways were about seven feet high, three feet wide, and five feet deep. The back half of each cage was enclosed to provide shelter as well as a private retreat and shelves for the animals' beds.

The scenes inside the cages ranged from pathetic and heartbreaking to fantastic and delightful. I was relieved to see that most of the cats seemed content. They dozed, dined, and delicately groomed themselves. A few broke my heart with their dull, listless stares or, worse, with insistent cries as they rubbed their arched bodies back and forth across the bars, begging us to pet them. But then I had to stifle a laugh at the sight of a large, cloud-white Persian cat who sat as majestically as a pasha on a red velvet, gold-edged cushion, her neck draped with multiple strands of pearls. Perched next to her on a camp stool, and daintily hand-feeding this regal cat, was her equally majestic owner, also festooned with pearls and "hatted" with a voluminous, floral turban. I raised my eyebrow at Nancy, who shrugged and rolled her eyes. "We get cats and owners you wouldn't believe," she whispered.

A few moments later, we reached the narrow alley behind Mikko's and Taiho's cage. As we entered through the rear, Nancy cautioned me to approach slowly. "Taiho gets a little nervous," she warned.

My mouth was dry as I entered the semi-dark, back half of the cage. I stepped past the shelf with the cats' towel-lined sleeping box and past their litter-box, tucked in a corner on the concrete floor. It gave off a faint ammonia odor. I stopped short in the entrance to the front of the cage. My breath quickened. Mikko and Taiho were dozing, curled together in a sunlit corner. My heart flooded with tenderness. How I loved those two, beautiful creatures! How grateful I was that they had each other for company.

"Mikko, Taiho," I called softly and tip-toed forward a step or two. Their fur stirred as both cats lifted their heads, their ears twitching and rotating toward the sound.

Then they saw me—and I was jolted by a pang of disappointment. I guess I'd expected them to jump up and rush to me the way children run to their parents. Instead, they stared groggily. Not a sign of recognition.

"Mikko. Taiho." I stepped closer, into the daylight. A spark flared in Mikko's eyes, but still she didn't move.

Taiho did move. At the sound of his name, his muscles bunched, and he shifted his body—*backward!*

I knelt and stretched out my hand. "Smell. It's me, Mikko," I murmured. "It's me, Taiho." Mikko craned her neck two or three inches to sniff my fingers, but Taiho backed off even farther.

I kept murmuring their names, and finally Mikko rose to greet me. But how slowly—stopping to yawn and stretch as she did. She eyed me with reproach and uttered a matter-of-fact meow. *Well, you've finally come. About time*, she drawled.

I was stunned. I hadn't counted on this kind of reception: One cat acts as if I'm poison; the other acts as if I've let her down.

Well, I, for one, was swamped with emotion. I'd be darned if I'd be matter-of-fact. "Mikko! Mikko! Mikko!" I cried and swept her up into my arms for one of our old affectionate nose-to-nose greetings.

Like a miracle, the hug shattered the barrier. As if she had been pent up and waiting for a sign, Mikko collapsed in my arms and began to purr, softly, then swelling to a deep, throbbing rumble. Her paws, pressed against my chest, began to slowly open and close in companionable kneading. Then, in a gesture that brought tears to my eyes, she raised her head to lick the tip of my nose.

For several minutes we nestled together, eyes half-closed in contentment. Mikko interrupted her purr just long enough to butt my chin and murmur in a low, loving growl. *All is forgiven. I needed you and now you're here. You are the most wonderful human on earth.*

In gratitude, I kissed her forehead. Then I turned to Taiho who was watching our love-fest with a guarded air.

"Taiho, come here, please," I begged. "Please, Tai."

I put Mikko down—she continued to purr and butt me—and edged toward Taiho.

And that was the moment in which I was utterly shattered. At my approach, very slowly, very deliberately, Taiho turned his back. The signal could not have been more clear. He wanted nothing to do with me.

"My gosh! Taiho!" Instinctively I reached to touch his back, but he shrank farther away, jamming himself into the corner. My voice was husky with emotion as, for the next five minutes, I crooned and pleaded. When I tried, once again, to touch him, he turned and spat! Not a fierce spit. He didn't bare his teeth. It was a show of irritation and annoyance. A warning: *You think you can sweet talk me after all these weeks. Forget it, lady. Just leave me alone!*

I sat back on my heels, too emotionally drained to even wipe the tears from my face. Mikko, with her sixth sense for my feelings, raised her face to mine with a bewildered gaze. She meowed softly and batted my arm with her paw. *I'm here. Don't forget that*, she soothed.

In his corner, Taiho curled into a hard, solid ball and stared stonily out through the bars of the cage. "Dear God," I prayed. "Please help him. He looks so miserable, so alone."

An hour later, still in Taiho's bad graces, I promised Mikko that I'd return soon, and I trudged to the bus stop. I was dirty and wrinkled from sitting in the cats' cage, and the dust of the road, mixing with my tears, caked on my face. I didn't care how I looked. I was desperate and thought only of Taiho. When the Gills had warned us that he wasn't adjusting as quickly as Mikko, I had expected him to be shy and wary, but not morose or hating me. I had been sure that at heart he'd be his amiable old self. There were still ten more weeks of quarantine! I groaned. What was going to happen to our lovely, lovely Tai?

"*Stop crying, woman, and think!*" I ordered myself. Wiping my tears, I made a silent vow to do everything in my power to recover Taiho's love of life and his king-of-the-hill attitude even if I had to spend long hours, day after day, in that cage.

I stopped for a moment, struck by a hopeful thought. *Maybe Taiho was angry because he missed his soul mate, Ward.* I pinned my hopes on that idea.

"Ward can visit only on weekends, silly cat," I muttered as if Taiho's sullen little face were there before me.

The weekend was two days away! With slightly raised spirits, I continued down the hill, visualizing the joyous meeting of the two good buddies.

It was a scenario which, in my mind, was cheerfully rosy—but, alas, turned out to be more of a very pale pink.

Nineteen

A Toast To Taiho!

In the soft glow of candlelight, Ward and I clinked our wine glasses.

"To Taiho!" we toasted.

It was a Saturday night, a month after our arrival. At the Third Floor, one of Honolulu's most elegant restaurants, we were splurging—celebrating a giant stride in Taiho's behavior.

True to my vow, for days and hours on end I had sat with the cats, trying to coax Taiho to come to me— or, at the very least, turn and face me. I'd become obsessed by the image of his rigid, unforgiving back. My only consolation during those heartbreaking hours was little Mikko. Her dependency and worshipful love had deepened. Each day she greeted me with joyous cries as she wrapped herself around my legs, her back arched, her head down, rubbing her face against my ankles, marking me as her very own. When I sat, she clambered up to nestle in my lap and gaze into my eyes with a melting look that implored, *Please don't be sad. I love you madly.* When she did that, I plunged my face into the thick fur of her neck and held her tightly.

The joyous reunion of Ward and Taiho on which I'd pinned my hopes did not happen. However, unlike his response to me, on hearing Ward's voice, Taiho turned toward him, and his shoulder muscles rippled slightly. At the same time, the tip of his tail flicked back and forth, which can be a signal of a cat's conflicting emotions. I suspected that Taiho was deeply lonely and would have flung himself on Ward except for his lingering suspicion that Ward was my willing accomplice in this miserable episode of frightening plane rides and endless quarantine. *The two of you are in this together,* that flicking tail accused us.

For three weekends, Ward sat next to Taiho, talking to him endlessly and lightly stroking his cheek. Although Taiho stared straight ahead and crouched as motionless as our bronze Egyptian cat statue, he didn't edge away. "He's taking his own, sweet time. He'll come around," Ward assured me. I was tired and discouraged, not nearly as optimistic as he.

Then, on Ward's fourth visit, Taiho made his move.

We were in our usual spots, Mikko snug in my lap, sleepily kneading my jeans, Ward sitting Indian-style next to Taiho scratching him behind the ears.

Suddenly Ward nudged me and gestured toward Taiho.

I looked and was torn between laughter and tears. Taiho's head was cocked, his eyes closed in seeming rapture, and he was butting his head hard against

Ward's hand. Moments later, as we held our breath, he
began to scrunch closer to Ward, finally wriggling his
way into Ward's lap as smoothly as flowing syrup. He
tucked his paws under his chest, coiled his tail around
his body—and burst into a rumbly purr!

"Thank goodness!" I breathed. My body slumped
in relief.

For a long time we sat in silence, each of us stroking a contented cat. For the first time our senses were
free to savor our surroundings—the fresh mountain
breeze that carried the scent of pikake blossoms, and
the sunlight, softly filtered by the rustling leaves of tall
palms. And, above all, the throbbing purr of two exquisite, sensitive, and affectionate Siamese. I'll never
forget those moments of warmth and love.

Finally, at Ward's urging, I stroked Taiho—gingerly
at first, offering my fingers to be sniffed as if we were
strangers. Taiho's nose twitched—would he reject me
again?—but he continued to purr. With a featherlight
touch I dared to stroke his cheek, then eased my fingers up behind his ears. Quite deliberately he turned
his head and stared into my eyes in the inscrutable way
peculiar to cats that convinces you that they're pondering deep thoughts. Was revenge on Taiho's mind? I
doubted it; Taiho wasn't a nasty cat, and his look,
though enigmatic, seemed to accept me. Or, could it
be a look of dismissal? I shrugged mentally. Whatever.
At least he hadn't turned away in a huff. Instead, his
head drooped, his chin plopped onto Ward's knee, his
eyes closed languidly—and this mysterious and discon-

certing feline was transfigured into a lovable, limp, and gently snoozing kitty.

From that day, Taiho gradually eased back into our family circle—at least for a while. We were overjoyed to have him back, but it saddened us to see that there was a slight change in his temperament. A spark was missing, the spark that had ignited his cocky, macho manner. And, although Taiho continued to parade rather than walk like common everyday cats, somehow his posture and stride just didn't have his former *Gang-way for me, folks!* attitude.

Macho or not, Taiho's "return" deserved to be celebrated with wine and fine dining. Besides, I must admit that we'd been looking for an excuse to treat ourselves at the luxurious Third Floor. We cheered when Taiho's giant forward stride filled the bill.

If we had only known what lay ahead of us, we might not have been quite so quick to raise our glasses in a "Toast to Taiho!"

Twenty

We Rescue A Damsel In Distress

While Taiho and Mikko occupied so much of our time and thoughts, unknown to us, there was a kitten problem in the house across the street, the home of Laura and Jack Sterns. We first heard about it when our neighbor, Jan, told us that the Sterns' Himalayan cat had had kittens.

I perked up. Kittens? Just across the street!

Jan's voice took on an angry edge. "Right. And get this—they sold one when it was six weeks old to a family with a four-year old boy!"

"Oh, no!" I cried. "Only six weeks old! It needs its mother. And a child that age doesn't know the first thing about baby animals!"

"Tell me about it," Jan snapped. "The kid carted that poor little kitten around constantly—practically choked it to death with a "love-grip." So now the kitten's back with the Sterns, but its mother and the rest of the litter won't have anything to do with the poor little tyke. She just huddles in the corner. The whole neighborhood's talking about it."

Sleep was difficult that night. We'd heard stories of mother cats rejecting kittens who had been taken away temporarily. We were haunted by this, and, before we knew it, we were talking seriously about buying the poor little thing.

"The question is—do we really need a third cat?" Ward wondered out loud.

"Maybe she needs us!" I replied with passion.

"And what about Mikko and Taiho?"

"I don't know," I admitted. "Maybe we should talk to the vet about it."

Ward bit his lip thoughtfully. "If it weren't for the fact that Taiho's improving so much, I wouldn't even give this crazy idea a second thought," he mused.

"We could at least just look at the kitten," I suggested.

Ward smiled wryly. "One look, and you know we'll be hooked."

And, of course, the next day we were. Hooked. Love at first sight.

Huddled in a fluffy white ball in a corner of the Sterns' screened-in porch, the kitten looked utterly forlorn. In the opposite corner her mother and littermates nestled in a companionable, purring heap. Hearing about the kitten's rejection had been sad enough, but actually seeing the gulf between her and her family was distressing.

We knelt, stretched out our hands and called softly. She didn't come. However, although she trembled slightly, neither did she back away. Her eyes, startlingly blue in contrast to her white fur, widened. They were wary and bewildered. My heart longed to embrace her, and I felt that she sensed our love, but that she held back for fear of once again being manhandled. I was almost blinded by a rush of anger toward the Sterns and the parents of the four-year-old. At her tender age, this kitten should have been romping and exploring, a bundle of curiosity, rushing to greet visitors, not cowering timidly in a corner.

"Try your famous magic touch, Ward," I whispered, half facetiously.

Inching forward, Ward touched the kitten's forehead. She didn't exactly fling herself at him crying out *My hero!* but she did stop trembling, and, as Ward massaged her brow, her look of alarm faded, her tense muscles visibly relaxed, and she uttered a tiny mew. Ward said it was a "thank-you" mew for the massage, but I suspected that that enchanting kitten was telling Ward that if he played his cards right, she'd dedicate her heart to him forever.

We ached to bring her home, but we still had enough sense (barely) to know that this decision needed much thought and a chat with Dr. Nathan, the vet at the quarantine station. He had taken a fancy to Mikko and Taiho and knew about our struggles to regain Taiho's trust.

We talked half the night but resolved nothing. Shuffling sleepily off to work in the morning, Ward wished me good luck with the vet as he kissed me good-bye.

At first, Dr. Nathan was skeptical, not so much because of Taiho, but because of the kitten's history of rejection and mistreatment. With a level look, he asked, "Do you really want to take on a kitten with potential psychological problems? No one wants a kitten like that."

"That's exactly the point!" I declared passionately. "What will happen to her? The family might give her to just anyone. Oh, Dr. Nathan," I cried, "if you could see her—the sweetest, most pathetic little thing! She needs love so desperately."

After a moment of deliberation, Dr. Nathan admitted that the best time to introduce a new cat into a family is before the original cats developed territorial rights to the house. Chances were that Mikko and Taiho probably wouldn't regard the kitten as an intruder. "You know," the doctor finally said in a thoughtful tone, "this just might work. Lots of luck with the little waif," he concluded with an encouraging smile. "Let me know how it goes."

I jumped up and startled him with a quick bear hug, then raced off to rescue the kitten. She'd have to get busy. Though she had already installed herself in our hearts, she had only three weeks to stake her claim to the household territory before Mikko's and Taiho's "invasion."

"Good news!" I shouted over the phone to Ward. "I'm going over to rescue her now!" Moments later, I bolted out of the door waving a check for $50 like a triumphant battle flag.

The kitten was sitting in her corner watching her littermates' rowdy tug-of-war with an old sock. Twice she tried to join the melee but was shouldered aside both times.

"Never you mind, little one. They're just snobs," I said, picking her up before she had a chance to duck away. I was startled by how tiny she was. Her long, Himalayan fur was deceptive, for, under it, she felt like such a fragile, bony, little creature.

Crossing the street with the kitten tucked close to my chest, I discovered that, compared to the swiftness of neighborhood gossip, the speed of light is a mere stroll in the park. Jan, spotting my dash to the Sterns, had called out to the kids in her backyard, that, thank goodness, it looked like the kitten was going to be saved! Whiz! Instantly a crowd of impatiently hopping kids greeted me in the cul-de-sac, morbidly curious to see the kitten who, they whispered all agog, had been "practically killed by a four-year-old." They bounced and danced around me with shrill cries of "Oh, let me see! Let me see! Wow, how tiny! Is it true that Frankie almost killed her? What's her name? Can we come visit?"

Upset with myself for not having the forethought to shield the kitten in a basket, I tried to tuck her head into the crook of my arm, but, frightened by the commotion, she squalled and bucked like a tiny bronco. Such a huge sound bursting from such a tiny body! And such fierce strength! It was amazing. Her eyes flashed with fear. As she squirmed to get free, it was almost impossible to grab her writhing body for she was as supple as an otter, and she clawed me as she tried to push off from my chest. The vibration of her straining muscles and the hard pounding of her tiny heart were alarming. My eyes stung with sweat, and droplets of blood trickled from the scratches on my arms.

Excited by the kitten's struggles, the kids squealed and hopped up and down like a clutch of jack rabbits.

That's when I lost it. I roared. "Stop! Stop it this second! You're terrifying her!"

The kids were stunned. Was this the cool Mrs. Morris who always had a chocolate chip cookie to spare for any passing child? They backed off fast, and I broke free of the gang. Still juggling the squirming kitten, I banged open our screen door and lurched into the blissful quiet of the living room.

I ached to collapse in a chair, but I didn't dare let go of the kitten. In her panic to escape, she might hurt herself or might wedge herself in the farthest corner under the sofa, and I absolutely refused to let her begin her life with us in such a state of chaos. I had to take control fast.

Forcing myself to take deep, calming breaths, I concentrated on soothing her, stroking her, whispering soft shushes. To create a quiet, womb-like retreat, I sank into a corner of the sofa and curled there with her in my arms. Instantly she plunged her head into the crook of my elbow. Although I knew that it was an attempt to hide and not a sign of trust, still, the innocence of the gesture touched me. I began to croon, as low as possible in my chest and throat. I'd read that kittens are comforted by the vibrations of a low human voice because it's similar to their mother's purring. Gradually her eyelids became heavy, though, for some time afterward her exhausted little body shuddered with intermittent tremors.

We cuddled together for the rest of the afternoon, completely worn out, both of us dozing on and off. When the kitten's tremors ceased, I turned her over to cradle her in my arms, belly-up, in part so that I could scratch under her chin, but mostly to teach her to trust and accept gentle hands on her vulnerable, exposed tummy. At first, instinctively, she brought her paws up to a protective position, the front ones curled inward, the back ones bent. The soles of her feet faced out, ready to kick and defend if necessary. Cautiously, I ran my fingers lightly across her tiny, oval footpads, then slid my stroking finger under her chin. She didn't purr—it was still too early, but she did stretch out her chin, and, soon her round belly heaved with a small sigh. The tension drained from her, and her paws dropped limply to my chest. I, too, sighed, and we both closed our eyes. The only sound was the light click-click of the monkeypod tree in our yard when the breeze tapped its long, cocoa-colored pods against the metal roof and fiberglass shutters of our Hawaiian bungalow.

The kitten slept for six hours, half-awakening, once, to give Ward a sleepy, drugged look when he welcomed her with a light kiss on the forehead. All evening we whispered and tip-toed in the faint hope that a long sleep would work wonders to restore the kitten's natural trust, playfulness, and curiosity.

It was a forlorn hope. When she awakened to new surroundings, she instantly panicked. As if pursued, she half-jumped, half-tumbled off the sofa. As wary as a trapped doe, she backed away, her back arched so high that her fur spiked. It was a comical sight, and if we hadn't felt such pity, we might have laughed. Such a small, fluffy, kitten trying to frighten us with a rigid, Halloween-cat pose. We retreated, and, by degrees she sank into a crouch. There she stayed until midnight, without ever taking her narrowed eyes from us, until hunger finally drove her to the bowl of food we'd placed nearby. Even then, she edged sideways to the bowl so that she could glance up to check on us between ravenous, snuffling bites of tuna fish.

Over the next two days, we gained the kitten's trust by the long patient way, as we had done with Taiho—hours of quietly sitting on the floor, inching closer to stroke her lightly, constantly murmuring words of love. We tip-toed about the house to avoid loud noises or sudden movements that might startle her into hiding.

The breakthrough came on the third day. I was reading. The kitten was by my side—not snuggled in but close enough for companionship—when, suddenly, with a queenly nod of her head, she nudged me.

"Oh!" My pulse quickened. "Are you saying that you're ready to be picked up, your majesty?" I murmured in a tone of proper deference to her gracious gesture. In reply, she hunched an inch or two closer.

With held breath, gingerly I picked her up, nestled her against my cheek and lightly touched noses. The touch did it. The touch of her velvety nose led to a collapsing softness and the flowing of tenseness from both our bodies. We found ourselves in a rare and wonderful state of silence and utter peace. From that healing moment, the kitten took over the territory. For a creature whose water bowl was bigger than she was, she was a powerhouse of energy. To our delight, she began to act her age, doing all kinds of wondrous two-month-old kitten stuff. She romped endlessly after dust motes, pounced from hiding places to pummel our bare feet, attacked the tassels on a sofa cushion, and made prodigious jumps to snare the ties dangling in Ward's closet. Best of all, she began to strut with a confident air as if she knew she had limited time to stake her claim to the house.

Only one thing disappointed us. Although the kitten gazed charmingly at us when we sat on the sofa, she never clambered up into our laps of her own accord. If we put her there, she stayed for only two or three minutes. We told ourselves that she'd come around in time.

The other problem was that she didn't have a name. "We can't keep calling her "kitty." She needs a real name," I declared. With their distinctive character traits, Mikko and Taiho had been so easy to name, but this kitten hadn't sent out any name vibes. We tried out so many names—Shy Violet, Bashful, Tiny. But not one made us cry "Bingo!"

Then, one miraculous Sunday morning, it happened. Why, I will never know, but the kitten, hearing us awaken and stir, scampered into the bedroom, clawed and scrambled up the blanket, burrowed under the sheet and, with a booming purr, nestled down between us!

We cheered! I covered her tiny face with kisses. "Victory, little one!" I cried. "You've done it—won out over your miserable start in life!"

And, with that, I knew that her name must be "Maile"—the name of the vine that the ancient Hawaiians used to drape on the shoulders of winning athletes to symbolize victory. We knew instantly. It was perfect. In our eyes, little Maile was a winner. Spirited. Plucky. Victorious. How we loved and treasured her!

The next big step for this little fighter was to win the friendship of Mikko and Taiho. They were due home in eight days.

We crossed our fingers, gave pep talks to Maile—and waited.

Twenty-One

Showdown At The O.K. Corral

Crossed fingers didn't help. Not one bit.

When Mikko and Taiho slunk out of their carrier into the living room to find a perky kitten parked there like the proprietor of the place, they were two, very testy, and unhappy campers. Their eyes narrowed, their backs arched, they glared at me. *Now what?* they snapped. *Who's this—this little thing who acts like she has squatter's rights—this puny kitten?* Their tone dripped with disdain.

Maile had greeted the carrying case with lively curiosity, eager to know what marvelous surprise might emerge. Now, too naive to be wounded by their scorn and knowing only that the gods had dropped two playmates into her house, she rushed to salute them.

Back off, kid. Taiho growled a warning.

Bewildered, Maile paused, but only for a moment. Her zest for feline companionship was too strong.

She'd been spurned by her siblings, but here were new buddies! With gawky, kittenish leaps, she bounded ahead.

I said—back off, Taiho intoned. He punctuated his warning with such a wicked snarl that Maile plunked down so abruptly that her tiny rear end bumped. Puzzled and pleading, she looked to Mikko. *What's with him?*

But Mikko deliberately turned her head in an elaborate pretence that this spunky intruder did not exist. As far as Mikko was concerned, Maile was a cipher. Her regal head raised in an attitude of otherworldly calm, Mikko gazed haughtily into the distance.

"Meeks!" I admonished her. "This isn't like you!" I was disappointed. I knew it was crazy, but I'd pinned my hopes of Maile's acceptance on Mikko's agreeable nature. I'd even had starry-eyed visions of Mikko mothering the lonely kitten.

I knelt next to her. "Please, Meeks," I implored her, "give her a chance. Look at her. Such a dear little thing." With an air of doing me a huge favor, Mikko tossed a cool glance at Maile. *There, I've looked.* Her shoulder shrug was eloquent as she resumed her distant gaze.

"My gosh, Mikko," I exclaimed, "why this nose-in-the-air business?"

"Give her time," Ward cautioned. "Deep down, you know she's really sweet."

"Seems like that's all we do these days—give cats time," I sighed. Before Ward could chide me, I quickly admitted, "I know, I know. We asked for it."

I guess we'd also asked for this stand-off when we decided, against all advice, not to shut Maile in a separate room when we brought Mikko and Taiho home. The idea of keeping cats separate is to introduce them gradually. They can smell and hear one another and touch paws under the door between them. We had decided, with crossed fingers, that Maile stood a better chance of asserting her rights if she faced Mikko and Taiho right at the start. It was asking a lot of her, to square off her three pounds against Mikko's and Taiho's combined 20 solid pounds—"Showdown At The O.K. Corral," Ward called it. Our concern had been that if we kept Maile out of sight, Mikko and Taiho would stake an immediate claim to the territory and boot out all intruders—especially feisty kittens.

For hours we tried, in vain, to negotiate a peace treaty. But Taiho wasn't just angry; he was extremely hurt, proof again, that for all his big, tough-guy demeanor, at heart he was sensitive and easily wounded—and now he felt threatened by this tiny stranger. When Maile moved toward him, he growled and hissed—nasty hisses with his mouth wide open, exposing gleaming, fang-like teeth—totally unlike our lovable old Taiho. We were stunned—and bombarded with pangs of guilt by our decision, which seemed more and more unwise by the minute.

On the other hand, intrepid little Maile, who could have passed for a tennis ball on legs, wasn't cowed, but seemed actually intrigued by this big guy's hulking, menacing manner. She was determined to win him over. Like a little yo-yo, with a constant stream of friendly chirrups, and a coquettish cock of her head—memories of flirtatious Petrouchka!—time and again she glided smoothly toward Taiho, then backed off when he hissed, but returned a moment later, radiating charm. She was cautious but not submissive—a psychological balancing act as precarious as any high-wire circus feat.

Mikko continued to utterly ignore Maile, to look straight past the kitten, to stroll by without a glance, as if Maile were merely paper on the wall. Passing Maile in the narrow hallway, Mikko danced a dainty side-step and slithered by, pressed like a shadow against the wall, with an uppity air of, *God forbid that I should have physical contact with that creature!*

Maile turned a puzzled frown toward us. *Whatever possessed you to bring home these two? Weren't there friendlier ones available?*

"Give it time, Maile. Give it time," I droned, mocking Ward.

There was one advantage to Maile's presence: Coping with her took Mikko's and Taiho's minds off adjusting to a new home. A cautious but quick trot through the house satisfied them that, compared to the quarantine station, this place was a palace—light and airy, lots of room to run in, and an abundance of geckos to chase. Their favorite bright-yellow cat-chow bowl was clean and ready for service, and, reassuringly, Ward and I seemed to be permanent settlers instead of occasional visitors. If only this annoying kitten would disappear, Hawaii might turn out to be a paradise after all.

But far from disappearing, stalwart Maile was dreaming up new tactics. Something more coy. After trying several beguiling poses, she finally settled on a position of supplication—flattened to the floor, her front paws extended toward Taiho, and her chin stretched flat out between them. It was a beseeching posture worthy of a master of yoga. Tiny chirps fluttered from her throat. Her eyes widened innocently. Only ten weeks old, Maile could have taught the great Olivier a thing or two about drama.

The coy act delighted us, but Taiho, who'd watched through slitted, skeptical eyes, wasn't buying it. With an impatient shrug of his shoulders, he rose, snarled, and marched from the room, his spine slightly arched, his fur spiked menacingly along its ridge.

I was filled with doubts. "I wonder if we should have rescued Maile?" I murmured. "Should we even have brought Mikko and Taiho to Hawaii?"

Again Ward urged patience. "They'll be fine," he declared. "We can't expect them all to break into the Hallelujah Chorus together in just three hours!"

His joking helped. I had to grin. Then I had to laugh out loud because Maile had turned to work her wiles on Mikko. Her tactic was to flatter Meeks by trailing immediately behind her as if worshiping at the hem of the gown of a goddess. Mikko responded with the disdainful, unapproachable air of a celebrity who's trailed by a persistent fan. But she couldn't shake the tenacious kitten even when she tossed annoyed hisses over her shoulder and even when, in a startling, very un-Mikko-like action, she turned to swat Maile across the nose!

For a moment I was upset, but then it struck me that Mikko's heart wasn't in those rebuffs. Her swat had been no more than a half-hearted cuff. My heart warmed at the knowledge that Mikko was too sweet, too good-natured to be really mean. Maile sensed it, too. Emboldened, she pranced about, batting Mikko's twitching tail. With great dignity, Mikko sat. She coiled her tail about her with care, gazed down her nose at Maile, then closed her eyes as if the sight of the impish kitten were too much to bear. But she didn't hiss, she didn't growl. Ward grinned and gave me a 'thumbs up' sign—there was, after all, a tiny ray of light at the end of the Mikko-Maile tunnel!

But what about the Taiho-Maile tunnel? So far there wasn't a pinprick of light. Ward started to speak, and I knew exactly what he would say—and I was right.

"Give it time. Give it time."

That evening, at the familiar call of "din-din!" Taiho, cloaking himself with his most authoritative "top cat" attitude, marched to the kitchen. He turned his back on all of us—on Mikko, for she seemed on the verge of tolerating the tiny stranger, on Ward and me for letting her into the house, and, of course, on Maile herself for her very existence. With great satisfaction and gusto he began to chow down from his favorite yellow bowl.

Mikko rose, stretched and strolled in. Why rush when all she would do was sit and wait her turn?

Maile, who had yet to catch on to the importance of Taiho's status, romped in and was about to dive into her bowl of kitten chow when it dawned on her that a nearby bowl, where Taiho was dining, offered another choice—adult cat food with a hearty liver aroma! *A buffet! What a grand idea!* Like a social butterfly, she scooted over to join Taiho. We froze. We saw it coming: Taiho defended his dinner with a hiss that could peel paint off walls. Maile staggered back. She looked genuinely surprised. She retreated to her own bowl— but with reluctance and a querulous look at us. *What is wrong with Taiho? And Mikko, for that matter. Aren't buffets social occasions?* (We were later to discover that Maile, while endearing, was not exactly a rocket scientist.)

We slept in different rooms that night. When Ward carried Maile into the bedroom, where she slept burrowed into the curve of his neck, I turned off the living room lights, bedded down on the sofa, and called to Mikko and Taiho. I heard soft, padding sounds but neither cat jumped up with me. Another call. No response. My heart sank. My bones knew that the cats hated me. They'd never again cuddle in my lap, never rub their noses to mine.

Then, as my vision adjusted, in the dim glow of the night light in the hallway, I saw the cats. They were looking for Maile. Shoulder to shoulder, like the Shore Patrol on the hunt for AWOL sailors, they prowled the room, sniffing into corners, behind chairs, and under end tables.

It finally dawned on them. That annoying intruder was gone! In a chattering, babbling rush of joy, they hurtled themselves at me and in rapid-fire Siamese chatter poured out their woeful tales. *The quarantine! How humiliating! Then that audacious kitten! And we seemed to adore her! How could we? Well, thank goodness, now she's gone!* I couldn't get a word in edgewise to tell them that they were mistaken. While kneading my chest as if pummeling bread dough, they chattered away, assuring me of their undying love. They snuggled and wriggled under my chin and over my face. Their purr hummed like a breeze in a canyon. They nearly suffocated me. I felt guilty about accepting all this love from the mistaken notion that Maile was gone forever. Well, we'd tackle that problem in the morning. For the time being, I was content and happy.

However, I fell asleep wondering: *Was this the only way to keep peace in the family? Living with closed doors between us? Or*—I shuddered at the thought—*would we have to find a new home for Maile?*

Twenty-Two

Shampoo And Blow-dry, Please

During the next three weeks, the cats' antics kept our emotions on a ceaseless rollercoaster ride. We clung to the hopeful fact that the tenseness among the three had begun to lessen a little, particularly between Mikko and Maile. Neither Mikko nor Taiho volunteered to sign a peace treaty, yet Ward and I remained optimistic. It was a shaky optimism but upbeat, nonetheless. We held before us the ray of hope that had pierced the gloom that first morning when, with held breath, we had inched open the door between the bedroom and living room. How would Mikko and Taiho react to discover that Maile was still there. Hiss? Snarl? Snub her?

Their reaction shocked us. They were almost civil! Maybe a night of snuggling and basking in my undivided attention had mellowed them, for when Maile loped out with a winning good-morning grin, the two of them merely sighed and cast me a look of gentle reproach. *You kept her! Without telling us!* they chided. I guess they forgot that they hadn't let me squeeze in a word.

That was the first of the rollercoaster emotions that plagued us in the days ahead. One minute, hope soared; the next, it plunged. That first morning was definitely a "high." Cheers all around when the cats met and didn't hiss, snarl, or box each other's noses. Later that day, we cheered again when Taiho only glared at Maile instead of spitting at her when she pranced around him with a "come-hither-and-play-with-me" glance.

"Good boy, Taiho!" Ward applauded and rumpled Taiho's fur, *mano á mano*, the way Taiho loved. Or used to love. Now, muttering who-knows-what-curses under his breath, the grumpy cat just shifted his glowering looks from Maile to Ward. Ward, the friend he had trusted, Ward, his hero, and now, Ward, the traitor who had opened his home and his heart to this brazen kitten with the long fur, fur that Ward and I thought was so beautiful. But just wait until it shed all over the furniture, wait until we had to constantly comb and unsnarl it. That fuzzy kitten might not be such a little treasure then.

To punctuate this diatribe, Taiho grumped deep in his throat. We broke into grins, for, as far as we were concerned, grumpiness was okay. Grumpiness we could handle. Grumpiness was much better than the vicious snarling of 24 hours earlier.

"Tai's going to be okay." Ward's tone was half confident, half doubtful.

"Yeah. Just give him time. Right?" I teased Ward to bolster his spirits.

But—we should have known better—we were too hopeful, too soon. We were due for a fall.

A big part of the problem was that Maile was so eager to win Taiho over that she was her own worst enemy. So, a short time later, when Taiho only scowled but didn't snarl at her, Maile figured *Hey, no problem!* and, with a joyful, running leap, she pounced on him. A bad career move. Taiho was not ready for joyful jumping. This time he hissed, he growled, he snarled, he hunched his back, rippling his skin ominously like a snake about to strike.

But Taiho did not strike. Taiho never struck. Deep down, he was just too nice a cat. And, as the days passed and his scowling brow softened, and his hisses faded like drawn-out echoes, our hopes began to rise. Sometimes, when Maile got carried away and flirted coyly within millimeters of Taiho's nose, he harrumphed and frowned and wheezed at her like a gouty old uncle. We sensed that his heart wasn't in this cranky behavior, but that he did it because the tradition of male Siamese cat behavior required him, at the very least, to put up a facade of a macho image. We desperately wished that he'd succumb to Maile's wiles, for, at heart, Tai was a jaunty, fun-loving guy. "Look what you're missing with this sullen attitude!" I protested to him more than once, because when it came to prancing and dancing, chipper Taiho could have given Maile a run for her money if he wanted to.

Then, out of the blue, Maile had a sudden, scary bout of diarrhea with scant but ominous streaks of blood. Tiny as she was, it quickly weakened her. As I drove her to a vet in Honolulu, the sight of her, huddled in a nest of soft towels with her head bent and buried in her chest, brought back sharp, terrifying images of fatally ill little *Neunzig* in Germany.

"I see nothing wrong," the vet reported. "I suspect it's stress. You say she's rejected by the male cat? That could do it."

"But she doesn't act stressed! She bounces right back at him!" I said. "I don't understand."

The vet shrugged. "It's the same with people. Look how many act like they've got it made but underneath, they're churning with stress."

Armed with a bottle of diarrhea medicine, I took Maile home to squirt the liquid through her clenched teeth with an eyedropper—a hassle, but the droplets that Maile flung with shakes of her head were tiny and pale yellow. They hardly showed on the tile walls at all. Compared with "administering" the big, blue, worm pills to Donner and Tristan, this was practically child's play. I tried to stay positive by focusing on the doctor's opinion that as the cats adjusted, Maile's tender tummy would calm down. "If not, you may have to find another home for the kitten," he warned me. More emotional rollercoastering.

The medicine was like a miracle drug. Maile perked up, groomed herself with care and resumed coyly courting her compatriots. Taiho, still stubborn and wary, hunkered down and eyed this little flirt through slits. His pose was as brooding and moody as a Brontë novel. But practical, resilient Mikko took another tack. She must have pulled on her thinking cap and slapped her forehead in a Eureka Moment—for she finally seemed to realize that, like it or not, Maile was here to stay. *Face it. This kitten, this pesky, sassy bit of froth, was going to be around for a long time, and she, Mikko, had better resign herself to it.*

And so, one morning we were stunned to see Mikko lower her proud head and deign to look down at Maile with arched eyebrows, as if sizing up what she had to contend with for the rest of her life. Maile, with a chirp of joy at being noticed, bounded to Mikko and rolled over on her back at Mikko's feet. *I'm yours to command*, she mewed in a manner so engaging she must have put in hours of practice. Mikko was not as enchanted as we were. Enchanted, ha! Mikko twitched her tail indifferently at the pleading little kitten. She may have resigned herself to Maile's existence, but that didn't mean that she had to bond with her.

We took stock of our situation: We harbored a grumbling male, his grudgingly accepting sister and a puzzled, wanna-be-buddies kitten.

That was the status of our household three weeks later when the phone call came—a stunning phone call from Seattle. Ward's father had died unexpectedly of a heart attack. Shocked beyond tears, we booked a flight to the mainland. We moved in a daze. My mind has blocked the mundane preparations—packing, stopping mail and newspaper deliveries, and so forth. But I do remember one thing very clearly, probably because I was so worried about it: I remember putting the cats in a boarding kennel. Although I would have a change of heart later on, at the sight of the kennel I felt somewhat better about leaving the cats. It was a small, blue-gray, cottage-style building with a garden. Quite cozy looking.

Driving there was a nightmare. In their carrier, Mikko and Taiho flung back their heads and yowled while, alone in a makeshift carrying box, bewildered little Maile cowered in a corner. Her silence chilled me more than the shrieking. I was a basket case when I finally handed the cats to the kennel owners. They welcomed the unholy three with such amazing calmness that I felt steadier on the drive home alone.

Our week in Seattle, emotionally and physically exhausting in itself, was capped by a miserable return flight. The plane, delayed twice, was packed with sneezing, coughing passengers. We dragged ourselves off in Hawaii with bone-aching bodies and sinus-busting headcolds.

Within minutes of yanking our bags off of the luggage carousel, Ward rushed to his office while I collected our car from the lot and headed straight for the kennel. I could hardly contain my jumbled feelings as I sped down the highway. I wondered if a stressful week in the kennel had driven the cats back to Square One. I hoped not. My stomach churned. I'd already used up my lifetime quota of stamina and patience. My heart brimmed with eagerness to swoop up the cats in a bear hug, but, for fear of what I might find at the kennel, my jaw clenched so tightly it shot pain through my temples.

At the door of the kennel, I took a deep breath and knocked.

Why were the cats so strangely silent? They had said nothing when I'd greeted them with kisses blown through the bars of their carrier. The eerie silence continued on the ride home. It made me uneasy. I had braced myself for an old-fashioned tongue-lashing for having tossed them in the clink. Instead, the car was as silent as the proverbial tomb. Taiho glowered at me with fearsome intensity through the bars. Mikko leaned achingly toward me, and when I looked her way, her eyes held mine with the desperation of a lost child. Maile, her eyes squeezed shut, was curled into a ball as tight and shielding as a baby armadillo. Her only movement was a sporadic quiver of her hide and a twitch of her ears.

"No problems. No sirree, no problems," the kennel manager had assured me when I asked how the cats had fared.

But, in fact, there were lots of problems—nasty problems that I discovered when I lifted Maile from her box and saw that her fur was dull and spiky. It gave off a pungent odor, an acrid scent as if she'd been sick and hadn't bathed for days. Tense, biting my lips until they hurt, dreading what I might find, gingerly I parted the fur on her neck. I was so horrified I nearly dropped her. Fleas! Hundreds of them! Maile's tender hide, as pale pink as a petal, was black and alive with pinhead parasites. It was as if someone had parted her fur and sprinkled her liberally with pepper grains—crawling, jumping, biting grains. The sight was revolting. My eyes snapped shut. A choked cry broke from my throat.

"My God, my God, my dear little Maile," I wailed. No wonder she had hunkered down as if besieged, with only her ears and hide twitching. She hadn't scratched because she didn't know where to start. Her whole body was a massive, maddening itch. In her misery she had curled up and closed down against it. I was outraged, absolutely outraged: I forced myself to inspect her. Once again I was wracked with nausea to see fleas swarming across her face and shuttered eyelids, seeking to bite the softest tissue.

I was so congested and choked with tears that I could hardly see. I was aware of Mikko and Taiho watching, warily, from the doorway. Sobbing, I put Maile down and, sitting Indian-fashion on the floor, I pulled them to me. Taiho responded reluctantly with rigid muscles, but at my touch, Mikko rushed to my lap, uttering soft chirps. She butted her head repeatedly up and under my chin with such strength that she nearly knocked me backward.

I braced myself to check for fleas. Over and over I plowed my fingertips upward through their short, thick fur creating furrows across their pale hides. I could hardly believe it. Not a flea! Then I grunted as I understood the reason. Why bother with these tough, adult hides when such a pink and tender one was so close by?

Still shaken, I filled a tub with warm water for Maile's first bath. I wore long sleeves because I was sure that at the first touch of the water she'd jerk into a clawing frenzy. Instead, with heartbreaking limpness as if her spirit had given up, she let me slip her into the water and simply sat there, a picture of despondency and helplessness. I squeezed shampoo over her thin frame, so fragile that it seemed that it could be crushed in one clenched hand. The water, soaking her fur, turned it into a slick, translucent flow that sculpted and accentuated her boniness.

And that's when my tears and fury overpowered me, for as I massaged her, the thin foam turned brick-pink with blood and was flecked so thickly with hundreds of dead fleas that it looked like a foul, crusted, skin disease. Maile's lovely little face was a mask of misery but she only sat there, uttering tiny mewlings, her body quivering. Now I knew what it means to have a shattered heart. And I knew rage—rage so powerful that when I clamped my eyes shut, I saw red.

It took an hour to dry and lightly powder Maile. I sat on the floor with the hair dryer switched on low, ruffling her silken fur and warming her pale skin. After a first skittish spring away from the dryer, Maile accepted—and actually seemed to love—the treatment. She began to purr! To my utter amazement, she stretched out languorously next to me to luxuriate in the warm stream of air.

It was a startling reversal, and it made me feel a little bit guilty because of the times that Ward and I had laughed about Maile not being a rocket scientist.

Well, maybe she wasn't, but this amazing little cat who had suffered debilitating diarrhea and bloody flea infestation was a marvel in her own unique way. Here she was, her adaptable little self, smiling and purring and even extending her paws in a beseeching gesture toward Mikko and Taiho.

Who knows what those two were thinking? They had been shaken by my violent outburst at the bloody shampoo. Since then, they had played their cards close to their chest. Poker-faced, they had sat side by side, like silent tomb guardians, watching Maile and me. After a while, Mikko lowered slowly to a relaxed crouch. I sensed that she might soon wriggle into my lap, but Taiho sent no encouraging signals. He moved only once, when Maile extended her paw toward him as if offering a peace pipe: He narrowed his eyes and set his shoulders in a defensive, taut posture that warned, *Keep your distance, kitten. Don't fool with me.*

"Oh, dear, dear Taiho," I whispered with a sigh. "How I wish you'd understand." I gathered him in my arms. He allowed me to hold him but remained tense. His attitude distressed me—as well it should, for it hinted at even greater trouble ahead.

Twenty-Three

A Glimpse Into
The Future?

"Hey, Taiho, get a life," I snapped. I was totally exasperated with Taiho. He didn't understand my words, but he caught my tone, and, giving me the cold shoulder, he walked out.

I shouldn't have been so impatient with Taiho, and I regretted the words as soon as they were out. It really wasn't his fault that I was exasperated. It was an accumulation of many things that are difficult to write about, especially Maile's puzzling and debilitating illness and Taiho's mystifying and troubling emotional problems. The memories of those events, particularly of Taiho's mental turmoil and our powerlessness to help him, are still vivid and painful even though they are somewhat softened by a bittersweet ending.

It seemed that the miserable week in the kennel had rekindled the sullenness of Taiho's days in quarantine. He reminded us of a bored teen-ager. He sort of hung out. Sulked. The only time he was talkative and cheerful was when Maile wasn't in the immediate vicinity.

To revive Taiho's low spirits, I resorted to bribery—a bowl of butterscotch-ripple ice cream. In the past, my cry of "Ice Cream!" had the same effect on Taiho that the Good Humor Man's bell had on the neighborhood kids. It brought him on a brisk trot to the kitchen, eyes alight and prattling about his passion for ice cream, especially butterscotch-ripple. *Cool! You are the greatest! You remembered my all-time, favorite flavor!* He stopped chattering only when his head was deep in the bowl, his nimble tongue lapping with speed, efficiency, and slurping gusto. Then like any well-bred cat with pride of personal appearance, he settled down for a thorough, refreshing bath. It was long and luxurious, a meticulous grooming of every inch of his body, including between his toes—as if he'd had a glorious wallow in butterscotch-ripple. Handsome and self-satisfied, Taiho was a pleasure to watch.

But now, at my "Good Humor Man" cry, Taiho slouched in, as if force of habit, not a zealot's love of ice cream moved him. He lapped methodically, without zest, without licking the bowl to a mirror shine, without a word of thanks, and without an after-snack bath.

Taiho's crusty disposition wasn't all his fault. Part of the problem was that we couldn't lavish the attention he needed, for, within forty-eight hours of getting out of the kennel, Maile was stricken by another harsh bout of diarrhea. Of course, we zeroed in on her.

To this day I hate to recall the image of Maile hunched in misery in the litter-box, passing runny, bloody stools. Far bloodier than before. She was bewildered by what was happening to her. When she glanced up at me, the quizzical expression on her kitten-face gave her the look of a forlorn waif.

I was heartsick—and furious. The cause *had* to be the fleas. I had already given the kennel owners a piece of my mind about Maile's appalling condition. They claimed to be shocked, and apologized profusely. I intended to report the situation to the health authorities, but in the rush and confusion of our return from Seattle, I never got around to it. But now, incensed by Maile's suffering, I felt like storming the place. Instead, I forced myself to calm down and concentrate on the most important matter right now—Maile.

Although the poor little thing was weak and in misery, each time she used the litter-box, she dutifully turned around to scoop small pawfuls of litter over her mess. I watched her sadly. It wasn't just Maile's suffering that touched my heart; it was her amazing tolerance. I wanted to rage to the heavens, but could only weep as I dabbed her raw little bottom with warm, damp, cotton pads. I found it incredible that when I cleaned her, which must have stung painfully, Maile looked up at me and purred!

We had used all of the diarrhea medicine during Maile's earlier bout, so we could only pray for her and do our best to keep her hydrated until the vet's office opened in the morning. Once again we separated the cats for the night. Ward settled in the bedroom with

Mikko and Taiho, who stared from a distance at Maile as if she had the plague. I put a fresh kitty-litter box in the living room and made a kitten bed for Maile next to the sofa. I spent the night next to her, dribbling water into her mouth from an eyedropper. Instead of clenching her teeth against the eyedropper as she had done with the medicine, Maile was grateful for the cool water. Her pink sliver of a tongue curled and lapped eagerly around the end of the dropper.

I must have slept soundly, at least part of the night, for I didn't hear Maile get up, but in the morning, I saw that she had used her litter-box, and I shuddered to find that her tiny rump was sticky with congealed blood. Worse yet, moments later, she labored to the litter-box once again, where, with her frail body heaving, she literally pumped out red-black blood. I moaned and went as limp as if my bones had melted. I was paralyzed with horror. Oh, God! I cried out for Ward. I was flooded with hot tears that swelled my eye sockets.

The foul blood seeping from Maile's quivering body was an abomination, an obscene image so vivid that it still haunts my memory. If possible, Maile became even more precious to us throughout her ordeal, for, amazingly, she endured—passive and, much of the time, actually purring.

During the next few days, with Maile curled and subdued on the car seat beside me, I drove back and forth several times to the veterinary clinic in Honolulu, ten miles away. I'm amazed that I didn't have an accident for the highway was just a big blur through my tears. The clinic, recommended by a neighbor, struck me as too large and impersonal. With reluctance, I handed the limp, submissive kitten to a receptionist. She, in turn, handed her to an aide, who took her away, presumably to hand her to the doctor, while I drummed my fingers or leafed, unseeing, through magazines in the waiting room.

I was disheartened when the doctor reported that the cause of Maile's illness couldn't be pinpointed. With growing despair I listened to him tick off the possibilities. Stress was one. But could stress account for so much blood? Tapeworms was another. The doctor hadn't seen signs of any, but inasmuch as tapeworm larvae can be carried by fleas, it was conceivable that worms could be in Maile's intestines. My throat tightened with revulsion.

The doctor went on. Maybe Maile was intolerant of her diet. Maybe she needed special prescription food. A bland diet. When he said that, I reeled. How would we handle that? Like most cats, ours were nibblers. They snacked throughout the day, like teenagers raiding the fridge. Their food bowls had to be available at all times. Maile may not have been the sharpest kitten in Hawaii, but, given the choice of Mikko's and Taiho's beef-flavored chow and a "special bland diet," of course, she'd beeline for the chow. It was as ridiculous as asking a five-year-old to choose his own dinner—a hamburger-and-fries or liver-and-spinach.

"But, you never can tell," the vet added. "Maile might actually like the special diet. Let's give it a trial."

"Ha!" I snapped. But we tried it.

The canned special diet looked—and probably tasted—like a lumpy stew of mashed chalkboard erasers. Maile's reaction to it reminded me of an old *New Yorker* magazine cartoon: A furious, scowling little girl, seated at the dinner table, kicks a table leg and screams at her pleading parents, "I say it's spinach, and I say 'the hell with it!'"

Of course, Maile didn't cuss. She was too well-bred for that. However, she defied us with an obstinate gleam in her eye and a jaw clenched tightly enough to grind gravel.

Every time we returned from the vet's, Mikko and Taiho rushed to greet me, but the second that Taiho saw Maile, his welcome chatter turned ugly, and he stalked off to brood in a far corner, muttering darkly and refusing to be touched or comforted.

But there was always Mikko—dear, beloved little Mikko who, I now realize, was coping as best she could with an array of puzzling emotions, desires, needs, and fears. With admirable faithfulness, she never forsook Taiho, even in his foulest moods, even when, in his throatiest Greta Garbo voice, he growled *I want to be alone*. I cheered her for her surprising determination to snuggle next to him and offer solace by grooming him with such fervor that he finally broke out in a purr—grudging and hesitant, but a purr, nevertheless.

Mikko wasn't always angelic herself, but many times during her 19 years with us, I swore that she took her orders directly from the angels: "You've been put on earth to make it a more wonderful place. Go, and be loving." And Mikko did her darndest to obey.

One of the few bright spots in those days was Mikko's increasing tolerance of Maile. She had vowed not to bond with the little intruder, and she didn't—at least not then. But she seemed to be more patient of the kitten. Because of Mikko's sweetness to me when I had headaches, I knew that she was an especially sensitive cat. Now I wondered if she sympathized with Maile's discomfort, for she had toned down her aloofness, and, once or twice, I even caught her nosing around Maile's face and ears. I smiled to see that Maile had the sense to stand stock still, eyes closed, as if aware of the importance of passing this inspection. Little by little, we notched up our hopes for a Mikko-Maile friendship.

But Mikko was also more and more demanding of my attention. Because she was so amiable, I'm afraid I tended to take her for granted. "Later, Mikko, later," I told her all too often when I felt harried by her loving eyes that fastened on me as she shadowed me around the house.

One week, to monitor Maile's health, the vet kept her at the clinic for three days. It was almost impossible for me to leave her there to endure more lonely days and nights in a cage, with strange hands prodding her with thermometers and needles. I had a powerful urge to snatch her and flee, but instead, I kissed her good-bye and drove home with an empty heart.

What a homecoming! When I walked in without Maile, Mikko and Taiho squawked with joy. They could

hardly believe their good fortune. But then they became suspicious. *Wait a minute. She has never come home
without that blasted kitten. She has to be here. Probably
hiding.* Raising their upper lips above their teeth in a
horrid grimace to show that they were deadly serious
about finding her, they tracked through the house sniffing the air as professionally as trained bloodhounds.
When they came up empty-handed, they skulked and
circled me with baleful stares as if I had stashed her up
my sleeve. "Not here," I declared, turning out my pock-
ets and shaking my sleeves. They exchanged a baffled
glance. Then it came to them! *The yard! Of course! She
was in the yard and would sashay in any second.*

Over their dead bodies. With the air of a couple of
cocky crime cops, they sidled to the back door and
pressed their noses to the screen. But there was only a
lazy gecko, stretched in the sun.

Finally, they believed. I had come home without
The Intruder! If they had been cats given to drink,
they'd have broken out the champagne. Instead, in a
prattling, chattering rush of joy, they nearly knocked
me over in an orgy of head butting, chin rubbing, chest
kneading, and twirling figure-eights around my ankles
with their sinuous bodies. I picked them up, apologizing over and over to Mikko for having given her short
shrift and, with happy cries of "Tai, Tai, Tai!" I welcomed the return of Taiho's amiable self.

When Ward came home, after checking to make
sure that he wasn't smuggling Maile in, the cats did an
encore of their joyful welcome. That evening the four
of us nestled and nuzzled on the sofa. It was the most

peaceful, contented time we had spent together since leaving Virginia. I reveled in it, but in the back of my mind was the disturbing image of little Maile in a cage—sick, fearful, and alone.

Later that night, Ward and I talked about the situation. We had to admit that without Maile, life was fairly smooth. Well, at least it was for Mikko and Taiho. But not for Maile. And not for Ward and me, for we loved that dear little kitten, and, rightly or wrongly, we had committed ourselves to her. We vowed to make this work. We were heartened by the progress in Mikko's and Maile's relationship, and, given Mikko's agreeable nature, we were fairly sure that it would work out in the end even if it took several weeks—or months.

The problem was Taiho. We had never imagined such jealousy or such territorial claim over people— *his family*—even without territorial claims to the house. We pledged our loyalty to that troubled cat and vowed to take him aside, alone, every day, and give him extra attention. Surely, he would eventually understand that our hearts were big enough for all three of them.

We knew that we faced long odds in bringing complete and lasting peace to the house, but our affection for all three cats was so deep that we were determined to give it a try.

Maile would be home in two days. Would she be healthy? After so much stress, would she still be an amiable, pleasant kitten? And--the biggest question of all—would Taiho come to his senses and realize that life could be wonderful if he would just accept Maile and, once again, take his rightful place as jaunty "top cat?"

Twenty-Four

Somewhere, Under The Rainbow

When Maile returned from her three days at the clinic, Ward and I received her with the same joy as did the welcoming father of the Prodigal Son. Her diarrhea had cleared up, and if we hadn't feared a relapse, we would have slain a fatted calf to welcome her. Instead—a bit of an anti-climax—we popped a fresh can of tuna-flavored kitten chow.

From the kitchen doorway, Mikko watched our emotional greeting with guarded, dispassionate eyes. Clearly she was reserving judgment of this situation. *Let's see what happens*, her body language said. But for the moment she was playing it very cool.

Not Taiho. He was as miffed as the Prodigal Son's jealous brother. Why such an enthusiastic reception for Maile? What had she done to deserve it? The three days without her had been great—terrific, in fact. And now The Intruder was back and everybody was catering to her. Taiho threw a disgusted scowl over his shoulder, and, pulling a cloak of wrath about his hunched shoulders, he stalked off.

"Our vow to lavish him with attention!" I cried. With that, I flew to Taiho, and, curling him around my neck like a fur collar—a snug, lofty position he liked—I carried him to the bedroom and plunked him on the bed for a session devoted to roughhousing, chin scratching, tummy tickling, and the promise of a bowl of ice cream. Extra large. Butterscotch-ripple, of course.

Taiho was skeptical at first and craned his neck to see if the prodigal had sneaked in behind us. When it dawned on him that this was his private session of horseplay and camaraderie, his mood flip-flopped. He grinned, he melted, pliant as a rag doll, and batted my cheeks with soft paws. Then, when his excess of loving energy was at the bursting point, he sprang up to butt and pummel me, chattering like an excited bluejay. Once or twice, his prattle became squawky, which I interpreted as major grousing about Maile.

I look back on that day with a stab of sorrow. It was one of the last times we were to share Taiho's boundless love of life, for soon after, Taiho's personality changed for the worse. He was like Jekyll and Hyde. When Maile wasn't around (we'd shut her in the bedroom with an armload of cat toys for a couple of hours at a time), he was almost his old self—playful and confident. But the minute she returned, it was as if a switch clicked in Taiho's brain; he became morose, sulky, and brooding. When Maile came near—for she still harbored faint hopes that he might play—he bunched his head and neck farther down into his hunched shoulders and squeezed his eyes shut as if he couldn't stand the sight of her.

In Maile's presence Taiho even spurned Ward, his one-time hero. Yet, the instant that she left, after checking to make sure that she'd gone, Taiho jumped into our laps and rammed his forehead repeatedly against our chins as if to drum into our heads that life could literally be the cat's meow if we would just toss out that prodigal, that intruder, that fuzzy pain-in-the-neck.

But we couldn't toss out Maile, and so, over the next couple of weeks, we watched, helplessly, as Taiho's listlessness intensified. He withdrew so deeply that he hardly responded to us at all, even when Maile was absent. He just hunkered in a corner of the living room. At first, he glared at us for hours on end. Later, he just stared straight ahead with an unseeing, faraway look. When we tried to comfort him, he grunted and turned away, exactly as he had done at the Quarantine Station. We were distraught to the point of obsession. We nearly drove ourselves crazy with "what ifs." What if we had not brought the cats to Hawaii? What if we had not rescued Maile? What if we had not gone to Seattle and left the cats in the flea-ridden kennel? Though we repeatedly told ourselves that we had tried to do our best for all three cats, we were haunted by guilt.

Besides the problem of Taiho, one other thing disturbed us: It was Maile. After her three-day hospitalization, she occasionally acted wary when we tried to pet her. Sometimes—it was barely perceptible—she cringed backward; other times she flicked out a warning paw. Once, she startled me by drawing a drop of blood. Naturally, we flew to The Book, and learned that kittens who make frequent trips to the vet may become leery of hands reaching for them. No wonder. To calm a nervous cat, vets will first caress and soothe it—then, bingo, they administer a shot or pop a pill down the kitty's throat. Maile had learned this the hard way and was taking no chances. We hoped that, over time, she'd learn to trust us unconditionally.

But that was in the future. Right now it was Taiho who needed professional help. Rather than drive all the way to the vet in Honolulu, we took the advice of one of Ward's co-workers and called Dr. Tanaka, who was recommended as "the greatest vet ever!"

Dr. Tanaka was a young, soft-spoken woman of Japanese descent whose love of animals showed in her eyes. When we called for an appointment, she surprised us by promising to come to the house the next day. Come to the house? She laughed at our puzzled tone and explained that animals respond better if they are treated at home, in familiar surroundings, instead of in a strange, stress-inducing clinic. And so, Dr. Tanaka brought the hospital to the animals! Her clinic-on-wheels was fantastic—a gleaming, fully equipped, custom-designed van!

The instant the doctor walked through the door, I gave her my heart, for when she saw the cats, she promptly sank to her knees, called softly to them, and offered her fingers for sniffing. For Mikko, it was love-at-first-sight. Within seconds, she was lolling about the doctor and pledging her devotion to this gentle, soft-speaking woman who was running her practised fingers up and down Mikko's spine, around her ears, and, caressingly, over her tummy.

Maile, curious, crept closer but flicked her warning paw when the doctor extended her hand. Hastily, and somewhat embarrassed as if Maile's behavior were due to poor upbringing, I explained the reason. Dr. Tanaka nodded. "She may outgrow it," she said. "Let's hope so. I won't touch her today. We'll let her get used to me."

Next, while we watched from the doorway of the living room, Dr. Tanaka moved toward Taiho. He eyed her, unblinking, from his crouched posture in the corner. She moved slowly, fluidly, and kept up a constant comforting murmur. My heart was in my throat. Taiho was so unpredictable these days. How would he react? Crawl away? Lash out at her?

He did neither. Instead, uttering low, broken cries deep in his throat—cries that brought tears to my eyes—he let her settle next to him and touch him with light, exploring hands.

For the next five minutes Dr. Tanaka examined Taiho in a leisurely fashion so as not to frighten him. She listened to his heart, palpitated his tummy, and checked his ears and eyes. We were amazed when he let her open his mouth and probe around his gums and tongue.

We were relieved to hear that Taiho was physically fine although I had halfway wished something to be wrong—something that could be treated with medication to cure his emotional problems.

In our distress we poured out our story and our feelings to this doctor who seemed so understanding. Immediately she sympathized and assured us that no one could have foreseen this problem with Taiho. She agreed with the opinion of the vet at the quarantine station: In most cases, the best time to bring a new kitten into the house is when the others are in quarantine. We had done what was right, she affirmed. Taiho just happened to be an unusually stressed cat.

Besides prescribing lots more TLC for Taiho, Dr. Tanaka started him on the first of a series of various vitamin supplements and anxiety-reducing medications, including hormones.

Over the next few weeks, Dr. Tanaka visited regularly, but despite all our care and love, Taiho didn't respond to any treatment. As the days passed, he sank deeper and deeper into gloom. His behavior became bizarre. Sometimes he spent hours stalking around the house, muttering angrily, without purpose or direction. Other times he crouched, humped, and miserable either in an out-of-the-way corner or, surprisingly, in the middle of the hallway so that we had to step over him. What did he want—to be isolated? To be the center of attention? We tried to fulfill his wishes, leaving him alone when he crept away and showering him with love when he seemed to crave attention. But his response was always a dispassionate stare or a grumbling turn-ing away. His behavior was unbearable to see.

Soon, Taiho lost much of his appetite. He seldom drank and had to be hydrated by Dr. Tanaka. His coat became dull, and he began to lick himself, constantly, almost frantically, until he wore several areas thin. It broke our hearts to see him in such terrible mental and physical torment.

Then, as Dr. Tanaka had warned might happen, Taiho began to spray, or urine-mark, even though he was neutered. From both the doctor and The Book we learned that cats spray because of stress. With grow-ing anxiety, they become extremely insecure and are driven by a strong need to redefine their territory. For-tunately, Taiho didn't spray Ward or me, but he did spray the stove and refrigerator repeatedly. I had never seen a cat spray before. I was morbidly fascinated as I watched Taiho walk deliberately to the refrigerator, turn his rump to it, raise his tail until it was ramrod stiff and quivering, and then spray a jetstream of urine. I was horrified by his act and disgusted by the foul odor of the yellow urine, which seemed to have a waxy flow as it dripped heavily down the sides of the appliances. And I was frightened by the intensity of feeling the action revealed. I sensed more than territorial mark-ing. I sensed spite. And I cried.

If Taiho wanted to punish us, he was succeeding. Strangely, however, the more Taiho displayed his an-ger toward us, the more we pitied and loved him. And so, when The Book advised us to shout, scold, and slap his rear sharply when we caught him spraying, we tried but couldn't do it. Why distress the poor creature even more?

After several weeks, Dr. Tanaka admitted that she had run out of options. "If Taiho were a human being, I'd recommend a psychiatrist," she said. "But he's not and...." Her words faded and she shrugged her shoulders in a helpless gesture.

We had been hoping that this day would never come, but it wasn't totally unexpected. We had endlessly analyzed Taiho's behavior over the past few months, from the flight to Hawaii, to the quarantine, to meeting Maile, to his second time in a kennel, and to the disruptive comings and goings of Maile during her illness. If Taiho had had to cope with just one or two changes and breaks in routine, he might have managed. But the cumulative effect of so many disturbing interruptions was simply too much for his fragile emotional state. It was time—and all of us knew it, though we hadn't said a word—to consider ending Taiho's life gently and with dignity by euthanasia.

We talked long and prayerfully with Dr. Tanaka before making the decision. When we finally did decide, she comforted us with her professional opinion that we were making the right choice to euthanize Taiho—and also to be with him at the end. With great sensitivity, she prepared us for the experience, explaining that she would inject an overdose of anesthetic into a vein. It would put Taiho into such a deep sleep that he would not regain consciousness. "It's quick and painless," she assured us. "And remember, Taiho will be surrounded by love," she added.

Once we'd made up our minds, we moved quickly. Although we were sure of our decision, the next morning our hands trembled and our throats were tight as we prepared for Dr. Tanaka's arrival by shutting Mikko and Maile in another room and spreading a clean towel atop the washer and dryer at one end of the kitchen.

After so many weeks, Taiho knew and trusted Dr. Tanaka and allowed her to lift him onto the towel.

She turned to us. "You may hold him and say good-bye," she said quietly.

Together Ward and I cradled Taiho. He didn't resist. He just gazed at us with unseeing eyes. We kissed his forehead. "Good-bye, sweet, dear Taiho," I whispered. Ward murmured Taiho's name and nodded to Dr. Tanaka.

She grasped Taiho firmly, and, expertly, in the blink of an eye, she slid in the needle. I was stunned for, within a few heartbeats, Taiho went limp in our arms—and was gone. It was so simply done, as if his spirit slipped quietly and easily away.

Instinctively, the three of us reached out our arms to one another, and for several minutes we formed a protective, quietly weeping circle above Taiho's body.

Dr. Tanaka had arranged for Taiho's cremation at the Quarantine Station. She volunteered to take him, but we wished to do it ourselves.

I remember lifting Taiho's body into the car. To this day, I can feel the limp, warm, surprisingly heavy weight in my hands.

Ward drove. Neither of us spoke. We were overwhelmed by having seen a life that we loved slip away—

by our doing. Despite all our assertions that we were sure of our decision, a wisp of doubt fluttered in a corner of our hearts.

It was a lovely Hawaiian day with the brilliant tropical colors of the lush foliage and blossoms sparkling in the sunshine. As we turned off the main highway and headed uphill toward the Quarantine Station, suddenly our windshield misted with the fine drops of a *mauka*, or mountain shower. These quick Hawaiian showers that waft over the mountain tops are cool and welcome and quite lovely.

Ward turned on the wipers—and we sucked in our breath. Ahead of us, brightening the mist with a glowing aura, above the mountains a perfect rainbow arched across the sky. We were driving directly under the high point of the arch, as if we were taking Taiho on a road that led to a place of mystical beauty.

Our shoulders slumped in relief, and tears blurred our vision as all our doubts dissolved. Without question, this lovely sign in the sky told us that we had made the right decision. Our beloved and treasured Taiho was finally at peace.

Twenty-Five

Cats Do The Darndest Things!

With Taiho gone, Mikko's world turned topsy-turvy. She searched for Taiho for three days. She wandered restlessly through the house, whimpering low in her throat and nosing into every corner, under beds, and in closets. We tried to distract her with an overflow of attention, but Mikko, who ordinarily could curl, purring, in our laps for endless hours, was restive. With a fretful chirrup, she sprang to the carpet to continue her uneasy roaming. With her lonely, puzzled expression, Mikko looked like a poster child for orphans.

Maile was also puzzled. Her bewildered expression made her seem tinier and more vulnerable than ever. She had already coped with so many changes in her short life. Now, tense with uncertainty, she wondered what was wrong. *Why was Mikko forlornly pacing? And where was the big blustery guy whom she had tried so hard to conquer with coyness?* Only his scent lingered. With her small body taut as if ready to bound away from a rebuff by Taiho, Maile checked all the out-of-the-way places where he had huddled, but he was not to be found. Baffled, the kitten turned to Mikko. She took to padding behind her in restive roaming. But Mikko, lost, distracted, and lonely, ignored her. From Maile's wistful look we suspected that she craved the merest crumb of attention and would have been grateful if Mikko had tossed even one aloof, haughty glance her way.

We were so busy and attentive to Mikko's and Maile's needs that our own grief had to be put aside during the day. It was at night when the routine cat-care chores were done—water and food bowls washed and refilled, kitty-litter refreshed, and cats' coats brushed—that we were suddenly hit hard by Taiho's absence. When I sat, cross-legged in the huge easy chair, for just a moment I expected Taiho to bound to my lap and snuggle in. In the next instant of realiza-tion, my lap—and my heart—felt sadly empty. As the days passed, Mikko would eventually stop her prowl-ing and nestle with me, but for now she could not be comforted. And Maile had never been—and never would be—a lap cat. She would lie by my side on the sofa and snuggle against my thigh, but now, trailing Mikko, she was too confused for that.

On that first night after Taiho's death, as Ward and I sat gloomily in the living room making a pretense of reading, I suddenly realized what was wrong. It was too quiet. As always there was music—a soothing Schubert piano sonata—but there was no cat eagerly reporting the events of his day. *Why would I miss Taiho's chatter now*, I wondered. He hadn't gossiped or prattled away with us for many weeks. Yet, suddenly, tonight, with an empty heart, I recalled all the years of wonderful, animated hours of talk and laughter with Taiho. Mikko had been part of those times, and she would be again, but it was Taiho's typical male Siamese boasting and "big talk" that had dominated those sessions. Now, for some strange reason, I longed to have that excited, squawky voice demanding my attention, scolding me if, horrors, I decided I'd rather read than chat.

With a wry smile, I discovered that I even missed Taiho's fierce jealousy of the telephone. How he hated that machine for stealing my attention away from him! I had only to lift the receiver and Taiho was there, bounding to my lap, angrily nudging the phone from my ear and bellowing for me to get off. Finally I had to shut him in another room when I made calls.

But most of all, we missed Taiho at bedtime; there was no big cat to walk possessively all over us, to poke his nose under our pillows, to nudge us to move over and make room and to tunnel between us, then turn in circles to precisely arrange himself in a snug curl in the crook of our knees or the hollow of our backs.

As the days passed, by gentle degrees we began, once again, to open ourselves to the beauty around us—the balmy Hawaiian breezes fluttering the pikake blossoms and rustling the palm fronds, cerulean skies, and sparkling sea—and the refreshingly beautiful, rainbow-lit *mauka* showers, which now had special meaning for us.

Mikko and Maile also gradually calmed, either for-getting Taiho or finally accepting that he would not return. We were pleased to see that, little by little, in their yearning for feline companionship, the cats turned toward each other. This was one of the gradual and subtle changes in both cats' personalities that Ward and I noticed in the weeks after Maile's arrival and Taiho's death. Mikko's craving for assurance and at-tention, always a strong need, now deepened to the point of her never wanting to be alone. Just being in the same room with Ward or Maile or me wasn't enough; she had to touch us or be so close as to be virtually a shadow. As I worked around the house, wherever I looked, there was Mikko, her body language pathetically appealing—one paw limply raised as if about to reach out to tap me; her upper body inclined toward me in an attitude of supplication; her ears were alert and pointed forward, her mouth slightly open as if she were on the verge of calling to me. And, oh my, did she call! I swear that she had saved all her chatter from the years when Taiho's constant prattle hardly let her squeeze in a meow.

With Mikko's soul mate gone, her attitude toward Maile changed from mere tolerance to a need for her companionship. After weeks of kittenish antics to wriggle her way into Mikko's good graces, Maile now found herself being courted, and groomed, and snuggled with. Ironically, now it was Mikko who usu-ally initiated the mutual grooming sessions.

As life settled into a pleasant, uncomplicated rou-tine, we had time to notice—and enjoy—the cats' personality quirks. Now that she didn't have to spend all her time dreaming up strategies to win over Taiho or pestering Mikko for attention, Maile could devote herself to her favorite activity—engaging us in games of hide-and-seek by crawling into hidden spaces and waiting patiently, sometimes for hours, for us to find her, which we did with cries of surprise that made her eyes gleam with delight. It was a joy to discover this impish side to Maile's personality, watching her plunge or leap, wriggle or scoot, down into her hideaway holes—not just "official" holes which all cats know about, such as wastepaper baskets, magazine racks, paper bags, and cardboard boxes, but "unofficial" holes which Maile discovered when our backs were turned—sock drawers, laundry baskets, suitcases, duffle bags, and even the tiny outside pocket of our hanging garment bag. To reach that, she had to leap three feet into the air and burrow her way into the tiny pocket which was only big enough for a folded umbrella—or a small Himalayan cat. I found her hiding there one day, snug as a baby kangaroo in its mother's pouch. When I gently prodded the pouch, Maile's little face popped out to peer mischievously at me. *Didn't expect me here, did you?* her sly expression said. In fact, I was no longer surprised to find her in any out-of-the-way spot, even inside Ward's winter boots or under his naval officer hat on the top shelf of the closet.

Actually, Maile *did* surprise me one day when I opened my knife drawer in the kitchen—and there was a very pleased Maile playing hide-and-seek amid the blades! When she tried to wiggle her way out to me, but found that the drawer was too shallow to move around in, her delight changed to distress. She mewed feebly for help. By the grace of God, I was able to shoe-horn her out without slicing her like a ham!

Because of Maile's penchant for tucking herself into small spaces far from the madding crowd, we suspected her of harboring a Greta Garbo gene that, at times, required her to be alone to brood and to think. Given this occasional need for solitude, it wasn't surprising that she totally flipped for the cat bed that we brought home one day. We bore it proudly, for this wasn't just *any* cat bed. It was, undeniably, the Cadillac of cat beds—a cushy, enclosed, beehive-shaped bed in a smart, navy blue with white polka dots and saucy white fringe framing the opening. We intended it for both cats, but once Maile set eyes on it—a soft, snug *hole!*— Mikko didn't stand a chance. And, true to her nickname of "Meeks," she didn't even try to shoulder her way in.

Over years of use, the bed became lumpy and mis-shapen with a distinct Tower of Pisa tilt. The fringe, turned gray and ratty, hung as limp as spaghetti, but for Maile it remained a snug retreat. Sometimes she curled up to snooze in it, a charming circlet of white fur. Sometimes she sat, relaxed and regal, calmly view-ing the world from the circular opening. Maile was a Himalayan Cream Point, and as she matured, her ears, paws, and nose looked as if they had been dipped in thick, country cream. Her downy fur was as white as whole milk. She was a lovely cat, and as she looked out from her enclosed bed, I'm sure that she knew exactly how fetching she looked, charmingly framed in the circle of white fringe.

The cats' regular, shared bed was a beige "donut" bed, as soft as a marshmallow with ten-inch-high sides. When they entwined themselves in it—Mikko dark, and Maile light—they looked as delectable as a bowl of marble-cake batter.

As she aged, Mikko developed some delightful idiosyncrasies. One day, when I replenished the roll of paper toweling on the kitchen counter, without thinking about it, I kept time to the music on the radio by beating the empty cardboard tube rhythmically against my thigh. Mikko was in the kitchen (gazing lovingly at me, of course), and as I passed her on my way to the trash can, I leaned over and, with the tube, beat a light tattoo on her hindquarters. What a response! Mikko rose, arched her bottom in the air, and threw me such a goofy look that one might think she was sniffing pure concentrate of catnip.

"You like being beaten?" I asked and thumped another tattoo on her rump.

Don't stop. Don't stop, Mikko moaned with a full-throttle purr as she shimmied her rear end to signal her joy. As I continued the rat-a-tat-tat, I understood Mikko's feelings. When Ward works the tenseness from my shoulders with quick, little chops, I want it to continue forever.

From then on, whenever I changed the roll of paper toweling and drummed the cardboard tube against my thigh, Mikko hightailed it to the kitchen for her ritual Bottom Beating. As she got older and skinnier, and her hindquarters got bonier, the tattoo took on a hollow, echoing sound. I miss that Bottom Beating sound very much, and although Mikko has been dead for eleven years, every time I finish a roll of toweling, I drum the cardboard tube against my thigh—and long for that silly cat to come running.

Our three years in Hawaii passed quickly. Ward's Navy duties, despite occasional "flaps," allowed time for touring all the Islands, snorkeling, beach picnics, and immersing ourselves in Hawaiian food, music and legends.

Under Dr. Tanaka's care, Mikko and Maile thrived. Their only problem—it plagued all cats in Hawaii— was fleas. We never had another invasion of marching armies of fleas, just a daily raid of a dozen or so, an advance scouting party perhaps, but we learned by trial and error, and our defenses were strong. Every day, faithfully, I prowled through the cats' fur with a microscopically fine-toothed comb to spot, snatch, and squash any flea that dared attack our precious cats.

After the combing, which the cats tolerated (they seemed to sense its importance), came the part we all loved—brushing the cats' fur. Psychiatrists should prescribe cat brushing as therapy for anxiety-ridden patients. There is nothing so peaceful as being in a quiet room, slowly stroking a soft brush down the length of a contented, purring cat, that is stretched out on the bed, totally trusting, her eyes closed, and a smile playing about her lips.

Another line of defense against marauding fleas included periodic "bombing" of the whole house. My mind has blanked out the exact details of those horrid "bombs." I vaguely recall ugly cannisters that released a foul-smelling fog of flea and flea egg killer. I dreaded "bombing days." I had to cover all plastic surfaces and countertops with newspaper. I cleared the kitchen and bathroom, cramming everything into cupboards and medicine cabinets—appliances, spice bottles, toothbrushes, and cosmetics. I propped up sofa and chair cushions to expose all sides to the fog. I closed windows. I snapped shutters. I placed several cannisters strategically around the house. I carted Mikko and Maile, water, kitty-litter, cat food, soft drinks, and a book to the car. Lastly, I raced through the house setting off the cannisters, one by one, holding my breath until I reached the back door and, gasping, slammed it shut—and took off for the beach.

At first, during the short ride in their carrier, both cats shouted and raged, but they soon learned that we weren't going to the vet—and besides, they loved the beach. Not that they actually set foot on it. No, for the comfort of us all, I parked the car beneath the palms in a small park adjoining the beach, raised the rear "third door" of the car (it was a roomy hatchback) and allowed the cats, on leashes, to roam around the interior. We spent delightful afternoons there with all the windows and the hatch open to the ocean breezes. We nibbled and sipped, we admired the glint of sunlight on the gently rolling waves, and were lulled into a doze by the sibilant washing of the surf. It was so peaceful that I almost forgot that, on our return, I would have to scrub down all the countertops and put the house back in order before releasing Mikko and Maile, who, after their taste of freedom on a leash in the car, howled to be set free from the carrier.

Every house in Hawaii comes with its quota of geckos, tiny, skinny lizards who can shoot up a wall or window screen in an eye blink. They keep the house relatively free of bugs, and I thought they were cute, except for their nasty habit of decorating window sills with black dots of gecko droppings. I was particularly fond of the one who lived atop the window frame in our bedroom. I worried about him and his buddies when I set off the flea-killer fog, but they seemed to have the sense to flee just before I closed the shutters. To my relief, I never found a dead or dazed gecko, and within an hour of our return from the beach, the geckos were back doing what they did best—teasing the cats. It was as if the house had been designed with built-in entertainment for the cats, for, with their teeth chattering fearsomely, like mighty hunters, Mikko and Maile had thrilling, if frustrating, afternoons chasing and leaping for the geckos. It was a grand time for everyone. Though they never came close to catching a darting gecko, the cats got stimulating exercise, and the swift little geckos with their mischievous eyes seemed to enjoy teasing and taunting the hunters, then scooting to safety on the ceiling.

Like clockwork, at the end of three years, Ward's orders arrived.

"It's Japan! Do you think you can bear it?" he teased, waving his orders at me.

Japan! The mysterious Far East! Where better to take two cats whose ancestral roots were deep in Asia?

Twenty-Six

Dried Fish And Cherry Blossoms

With their heads deep in the food bowl, Mikko and Maile chowed down heartily, then used the litter-box—nothing unusual except that they were in the back seat of a mini-van barreling along a highway in the outskirts of Tokyo! Shades of Trushkie, our car-riding German cat who had earned her wings, so to speak, by eating and attending to her toilette on the autobahn at 120 kilometers an hour! These two could match her, kilometer for kilometer.

Once again we had lucked out. Here in Japan, where Ward would be stationed at Camp Zama, our sponsors, Jacquie and Tom Zmurko, like Julie and Dave Gill, were cat lovers. When our plane from Hawaii touched down at Narita International Airport, a three-hour drive from Zama, the Zmurkos greeted us with hearty words of welcome and piled us into their van. Jacquie and Tom could have given hospitality lessons to Martha Stewart. After the long, cramped flight, we nearly wept on their shoulders with gratitude, for they had brought sandwiches, coffee, cat food, water, and kitty-litter. (This time the cats and we traveled in the same plane—and, hallelujah! Japan has no quarantine restrictions!)

My heart had been in my throat when the cats' crate rumbled off the conveyor belt at Narita. How had they tolerated the long flight from Hawaii? Would they be total basket cases? It was deathly quiet in the crate. I held my breath as I peered through the wire screen— and beheld four of the widest, most bewildered, blue eyes in the world.

"Mikko! Maile!" I cried. Instantly they recognized me and answered with equal joy—such enthusiastic, loud, squawky joy that half the terminal spun in shock toward the noise. I laughed. They were fine. Somewhere along the line—maybe all those miles and hours in the hatchback—the cats had become seasoned travelers. I suffered a momentary pang as I suddenly thought of Taiho who, most certainly, would have either scolded or scorned us.

Thanks largely to Jacquie and Tom's welcoming reception, these two travelers loved Japan immediately. No wonder, like Trushkie who had been fussed over and admired in Germany (at least until her unladylike behavior at the castle-inn was frowned upon), Mikko and Maile utterly captivated the Japanese. Pet cats were rare in Japan, and pure-bred ones were expensive.

There is a charming "lucky cat" tradition in Japan; many bar and restaurant owners put a brightly painted porcelain cat statue in their entryway. The cat, sitting upright, raises a paw to summon customers inside. These are *Maneki-neko* or Beckoning Cats.

Mikko and Maile didn't perch on our doorstep beckoning to passing Japanese, but they were a great hit with our many Japanese guests. Maile's lush fur was stroked and admired, and, as the namesake of the Royal Princess Michiko, Mikko could have had the treasures of Japan laid at her feet had she desired it. But her tastes were simple, and she required nothing more than nibbles of tiny dried fish, preferably if they were offered by the gentle, shy, giggling, Japanese teen-age girls who belonged to our Intercultural Club. Both cats became addicts of these fish, thanks to weekly "present-o's" from our cat-loving maid, Emi-san. Silvery, crispy, about the size of a large paper clip, the fish were so sliver-thin that they looked as though they'd been flattened by the Bullet Train. To me, their smell was Concentrate of Dead Fish Fertilizer; to the cats it was Gourmet Heaven. When Emi-san waved the open bag of fish before the cats' quivering nostrils, their eyes glazed over. I could identify with their rapture, for my own nose had twitched like an excited bunny's the first time I sniffed the chocolate factory in Hershey, Pennsylvania. One big difference: Hershey Kisses left our mouths sweet and sensual; the dried fish left the cats' breath… well, let's just say that it was a strong incentive for me to brush those pointy little teeth with regularity.

During our stay in Japan, Mikko's and Maile's companionship deepened. I suspect that they turned to one another because I was rarely home. Plunging into Japan, I took Japanese language lessons, gave English lessons at Fuji Xerox Corporation, and, after cramming myself with Japanalia, I wrote articles about Japan for an English-language newspaper for tourists.

While I rushed about madly, soaking up Japanese culture, Mikko and Maile, perhaps because of their oriental heritage, seemed to absorb the essence of the country simply by reclining on the window sill and gazing out at the Japanese landscape. Unlike our first, dreary, military housing in Germany, our government housing at Camp Zama was a fine home on a hilltop with views over the valley. The expanse of sloping lawn was shaded by pine trees whose branches drooped gracefully with winter snows, with luxuriant maples that flamed red and gold in autumn, and a hillside of flowering cherry trees whose pink petals swirled through the air in the spring breezes as thickly as snow in a glass globe. It was easy to imagine that we lived in an ancient, Japanese scroll painting.

Musing on this landscape day after day, the cats quickly became attuned to the spirit of the country. Mikko acquired the typical Japanese affinity for water, which has an important role, both practical and contemplative, in Japanese life. It bubbles in big, old, tin tea kettles in farm kitchens and in the corners of tiny, family-owned fruit and vegetable stalls; it burbles and pours soothingly in quiet tea ceremonies; in manicured Japanese gardens it gurgles and rushes melodiously in streams over precisely placed pebbles; it provides a clear, ice-cold bath for blocks of creamy *tofu* in spotless stainless-steel tanks, and, during rains, from tiled rooftops, it courses in a silken flow down thick chains of dark, woven rope.

Shortly after our arrival in Japan, Mikko, with her newfound Japanese sensibility, suddenly became quite monk-like in her contemplation of water. Not a burbling woodland stream—but bath water, of all things! Well, when you're confined to the house, you make do with what you have. And what Mikko had was a bathtub with a very broad rim—the first rim we ever had that was broad enough for her to perch on. My baths became a highlight in Mikko's day. At the sound of the running water, she hurried to leap to the rim to sit in eerie stillness and stare pensively into the watery depths. Fittingly, there was a Zen-like quality to her meditation. If I circled my toe underwater, causing a mini-whirlpool, Mikko's trance deepened, and in a state of reverie, she dipped her slim paw to the water's surface—barely touching—then delicately licked the droplets that clung like tiny, diamond chips to her dark fur. She moved with oriental calm befitting a traditional Japanese tea ceremony. Her mood broke only when I, in typical *gaijin* (foreign) fashion, splashed and lathered and clouded the water with soap. Wrinkling her nose, Mikko leaped to the floor and hastened away from such crude, noisy, Western activity.

Maile hated water. She was a vain little thing, and I think that she knew she was not at her best when her fur was water-bedraggled. Zen-like meditation over water, whether still or moving, was not for her. Instead, Maile expressed her oneness with Japan by communing with nature, which she did on our secluded hilltop where we occasionally allowed her to stroll—chaperoned, of course. (Mikko preferred to assimilate Japan strictly through the window.) Maile's communion with nature was not as pure as it might have been, for it had a touch of vanity. She "communed" by posing against exotic natural backdrops. In the fall, she knew instinctively that the carpet of autumn leaves was a bright mosaic, against which, her white fur looked absolutely smashing. She stretched her hind legs languorously like a dancer warming up, perfectly aware of the elegant contrast of the kaleidoscope of autumn colors with her cream-and-white beauty. In the spring, she made it a point to stroll regally through the swirl of blowing cherry blossoms, casting sly glances over her shoulder to make sure that we were admiring her elegance. Indoors, with an uncanny sense of design, every afternoon Maile sprawled with languid grace on our jewel-toned oriental carpet in the golden light of the late sun. The effect was exquisite—an opulent, museum-quality, oriental still life. This cat *was* Japan.

From time to time, if too many of Maile's admirers clustered around her, she seemed to have a flash of kittenhood memories of hands reaching to poke and prod her and give her shots, and she reacted with unexpected feistiness. With an irritated swish of her plumed tail, she drew back a bit, then flicked out her paw in warning. Sometimes she retreated, preferring to view the scene—and be admired—from afar. Sometimes, skewered by her silent, distant stare, I wondered what she was thinking. Making mental notes of our lifestyle for a "tell all" bestselling novel?

Maile's occasional withdrawal into her private cat world lent her an aura of mystery that made her a more complex and intriguing, cat. I yearned to smother her with hugs and kisses but I respected her need for seclusion. It was, in fact, appropriate to the Japanese lifestyle. Every day I saw similar withdrawals in the crowded trains where the Japanese, crammed shoulder to shoulder, retreated to private, inner harbors.

While Ward and I respected Maile's sporadic periods of introspection, we chuckled lovingly at Mikko who, at all times, wore her heart on her sleeve and whose craving for affection, attention, hugs, and constant reassurance was touching. She was so mild-mannered, so "not" brave and so dependent on us that more and more we found ourselves using her nickname—"Meeks."

Our time in Japan sped by. We loved it. When we left, I cried. The only thing I wouldn't miss were the fleas. Yes, fleas! I thought that we'd said *sayonara* to them in Hawaii, but, early on at Zama, some Japanese fleas jumped both cats. They didn't invade in plague-like multitudes as did Hawaiian fleas, but they were persistent, and hung on even as late as cold November. The only good thing—a dubious good—was that our nightly deflea-ing and fur brushing became a relaxing time of togetherness for the cats and us. They stretched on our laps, up-ended their tummies, and purred their pleasure of Ward's and my company.

When, in October, 1983, we loaded the cats into the big, sturdy carrier and trundled them off to Narita Airport, the seasoned travelers shot us a questioning but resigned, look. *Good grief! We're off again? Where to now, guys?*

"Home," we said. "The United States. Virginia."

Like a magnet, once again, the Navy was pulling Ward back to the Washington, D.C., area.

Twenty-Seven

Grow Old Along With Me, The Best Is Yet To Be

— *Robert Browning*

If there's such a thing as a flea grapevine, my reputation as a no-holds-barred bomber and killer of fleas must have sped ahead of us via the vine to Virginia. Not a flea dared show its face to plague Mikko and Maile. What pleasure to comb and brush the cats without peering, eagle-eyed, ready to pounce on nasty, black specks playing hide-and-seek in their fur. Fur-brushing sessions became a gift of companionship, love and complete relaxation. And, as the years passed, relaxing, spelled s-n-o-o-z-i-n-g, became Mikko's and Maile's favorite pastime. Eventually Mikko's most strenuous activity was to flop from side to side in a patch of sunlight to make sure of getting toasty warm all over. Geckos could have skittered past—*sauntered* past—without fear of losing life or limb.

Besides snoozing and snuggling with us, eating was one of Mikko's passions, and, at my cry of "din-din!" she roused herself to beeline to her food dish. No matter how old Mikko got, she didn't miss a meal even when, at age 19 1/2, she wasn't able to "beeline." But she could totter—and totter she did, albeit on a somewhat uneven course, to her food bowl.

As luck would have it, Ward's work kept us in the Washington area for many years. With our "gypsy days" behind us, we began to put down roots. Our first root was a brand-new house. Mikko and Maile checked it out more thoroughly than the County Housing Inspector. We followed as they explored the empty rooms and ran down their checklist of necessary amenities. Big windows on both the east and west to let in the morning and afternoon sun? Check. A fireplace with a brick hearth for wintry evenings? Check. A deck where we can enjoy the great outdoors without actually getting dirt on our paws (vain Maile so disliked soiling her fur)? Check. A carpeted staircase where, in her solitary moods, Maile could perch on the top step to observe the social scene below? Check. And an unexpected, excellent feature—a nook under the kitchen counter that was exactly the right size for food and water bowls and two cats! No more chowing down underfoot in small kitchens! *How thoughtful!* they remarked in a vibrant purr, bestowing their seal of approval.

The first time that the cats dined, their tails, one
dark and sinuous, the other a white plume, trailed out
of the nook onto the kitchen floor, but getting stepped
on once or twice taught them a lesson, and they swiftly
tucked their tails in. After that, they took their meals
in blissful peace at their secluded "table for two." In
appreciation for this dream house and private dining
room, the grateful cats revved their purrs to Harley
Davidson roars, arched their backs like Halloween cats,
snapped their tails to tall attention, and wound themselves around our ankles as tightly as sailors' knots.

As the years passed, we discovered the pleasures of
living with older cats. A woman once told me that she
was a "kitten person." She adored the antics of kittens
but had "no use for stodgy old cats." I was so angry
that I had to bite my tongue. And yet, I felt sorry for
her, for she'd never know the companionship, the quiet
times, and the abiding love between cats and their human families, which deepen through the years—a relationship as comfortable and soothing as a favorite,
well-worn sweater, one that is treasured no matter how
threadbare.

As Mikko aged, she didn't exactly become threadbare, but we began to notice subtle changes. Then, one
day, when she was 16 and was snoozing in my lap, I
suddenly realized how much her appearance had al-
tered. Thanks to her love of food and her lack of exercise, Mikko had grown plump. Her warm, soft body
overflowed my lap. Her coat, which had darkened over
the years, had lost much of its rich gloss. It was spikier
and speckled with gray especially around her face. Her

eyes, once a clear blue, had begun to cloud over. I gazed at her with a wistful smile. I loved her so much. Seeing how she had aged made me face the fact, however reluctantly, that we might not have her too much longer. And so I put aside the book I'd been reading when Mikko had scrambled, somewhat heavily, into my armchair, and, with a nudge of her head and a plaintive mew, had asked me to shift a bit to provide a hollow in my lap where she could snuggle. When I did, my own body calmed as I watched her face and limbs go slack, her eyes close in repose and her sides gently rise and fall in slow steady breaths. Her paws became so limp and floppy that I could flip them with my fingertips like little pom-poms. This was one flaked-out cat. Then I chuckled, for Mikko's lips parted slightly and the tip of her tongue peeked out, as pink as a tidbit of salmon—a classic sign of complete relaxation and a perfect example of a cat that totally loves and trusts you and gives herself wholly to your care. Gazing down at her, my sight grew misty.

Maile, who lived to be 13, never appeared to age, perhaps because her fur was white to begin with, and she was always a small cat, so, in our eyes, she remained kittenish, especially when she rolled in the sunlight and her fur frothed up like a shaken feather duster. Early on, we'd accepted the fact that Maile was not a rocket scientist. Nevertheless, she was a complex little thing: sometimes, in a kittenish guise, she gazed at us with waif-like bewilderment; other times, when she withdrew into her private cat world at the top of the stairs, she had an aura of mystery and intrigue, and sometimes, in her feisty moods when she threatened to slap the hand that pet her, she narrowed her eyes striving for a villainous frown. But she never could look really roguish because, regardless of her mood, Maile always had a hint of that woebegone, wistful look that had shattered our hearts the first time we saw her, alone and apart, in Hawaii.

As Mikko aged, she discovered, to her utter disgust, that she could no longer balance all four paws on the edge of the kitty-litter box. She had to actually step into that damnable litter! We sympathized with her dilemma, but we had to laugh--not to her face, of course—when she solved her problem by rising up on tip-toe. On the tiniest point of her toes, like a ballet dancer, she stepped into the litter-box. With her hunched shoulders and high-arched back, her posture reminded us of comic strip characters who tip-toe furtively into the house, shoes in hand, after a late-night-out with the boys. With only four tiny paw points touching the litter, Mikko seemed to hover above the box, like a boat that hovers above the water on jets of air.

You'd think that after living with Mikko for 16 years I'd have known not to count her down-and-out the day that I noticed how old and gray she looked. Mikko was a survivor. She'd proven it, time after time. Now, that dear cat hung on for three-and-a-half more years. Not surprisingly, by that time we were on a first name basis with several veterinarians who specialized in feline diseases of the heart, kidneys, eyes, and ears, for Mikko eventually succumbed to most of the common, "older cat" health problems. Yet, she trundled on, living the good life and filling Ward and me with an abundance of love.

When she was 17, Mikko's heart specialist, in awe-struck tones, announced that Mikko was a Wonder Cat. Her heart *never* beat evenly. In fact, sometimes it forgot to beat for several seconds at a time! The news alarmed us, but Mikko took it calmly and didn't let it interfere with her lifestyle—naps in the sun, naps in our laps, naps entwined with Maile, and meals of soft, warmed foods. With advancing age and tooth loss, Mikko was particular about her meals. They had to be soft. They had to be microwaved to an exact degree of warmth. And they had to be served ON TIME. If all these conditions weren't met, Mikko let us know about it with her unique Siamese cry. No, not a cry. A scream. A Siamese scream without equal. Mikko's legs may have become creaky, but her lungs were bellows of raw leather.

About this time, Maile, at age eleven, began to change—radically. Shedding her role as aloof observer of the social scene, Maile abandoned her solitary post on the top step, joined the rest of the gang, and began to trot like a puppy after Ward and to SCREAM for his attention the instant that he walked in the door. What had happened? When we were out of the house, had Mikko taken it upon herself to pass on the wisdom of her old age and to coach Maile in the finer points of The Scream? Did she remind Maile of the proverb that "the squeaky wheel gets the oil"—that a cuddly, atten-tion-demanding cat leads a richer life than a feisty, aloof one? If so, Maile took the advice to heart. She developed a scream and wide-eyed pleas for attention that were masterful. Yes, Maile definitely was a complex cat, and now she was mellowing and improving with age. We'd always loved her, even in her Greta Garbo moods of solitude, but it was much easier to love a cat that loved you back with such incredible zest.

We nearly lost Maile when she was 12, due to an intestinal blockage—and we got to know another specialist on a first-name basis. The poor little thing had to have a series of horrid enemas that caused her to lose a fifth of her weight—and she was not much bigger than a snowball to start with! It was frightening to hold her scraggly, limp body and to feel her loose skin and brittle bones. Fortunately, the cat internal specialist was a miracle worker. For a fee almost equal to our mortgage payment, he fixed Maile up. Worth every cent; she rebounded better than ever—practically kittenish.

Meanwhile, Mikko continued to astound medical science. From a 17-year-old Wonder Cat, she went to 18-year-old Miracle Cat, and, at 19, everyone was calling her The Death-Defying Cat. Rolled up like an escargot in a patch of sunlight, despite kidneys as riddled as Swiss cheese and a tiny cancer on the tip of her tail, she would peer contentedly at us through cloudy, milky eyes. She could no longer hear the can opener, but her purrer continued to work perfectly, and she cranked it to top volume at the drop of a fond look. It seemed to confirm what all the vets assured us: She was a pain-free and contented kitty.

And then, one morning, Mikko tottered into the kitchen on spindly, unsteady legs, coming toward me as if she needed help. A moment later, as I watched her struggle to stay upright, her wobbly hind legs crumpled, and she collapsed in a soft heap. I will never forget the lost, confused look on her face as she raised her cloudy, bewildered eyes to mine. I couldn't help her. I couldn't explain to her that she was having a stroke. I could only kneel next to her, bend my face to hers, and tearfully tell her how much I loved her.

That afternoon, we held Mikko for the last time. Amazingly, she purred in our arms until our vet gently put her to sleep.

Ward dug a hole next to the woodpile in the woods behind our house while I fashioned a cross from small branches and strips of undyed cloth. We wanted Mikko's grave to be simple and natural. We buried her in the late afternoon with tearful prayers of thanks to God for having given us the blessing of her long, sweet life. We remembered driving toward the rainbow on the day of Taiho's death. And then we smiled. Mikko didn't need a rainbow. Mikko *was* a rainbow.

Maile lived on for two more years. Mikko had trained her well in the art of being irresistible and charming. Although Maile never did become a lap cat, she was skilled in burrowing deep into the sofa cushions next to us. We got used to that little purring bundle of warmth against our thighs.

When Maile was 13, we put her to sleep when an undiagnosable illness wore her down to a shadow. I fashioned another cross of rough branches, and we offered more prayers for the gift of little Maile. Before we buried her in a towel-lined box, I clipped a tuft of hair from Maile's cheek. I keep it in a velvet-lined silver box. It looks like a small, pure-white, curved feather. When, occasionally, I brush the "feather" lightly over my own cheek, I sense her delightful presence briefly once again.

Ten years have passed. The graves have crumbled and returned to the soil. When I look from my kitchen window into the woods, I don't see a trace of them. But the cats—all eight of them—live on vividly in our memories and in our hearts.